DATE DUE

THE TASTE OF OUR TIME

Collection planned and directed by

ALBERT SKIRA

BIOGRAPHICAL AND CRITICAL STUDSTUDY

BY

LIONELLO VENTURI

Translated by James Emmons

PIERO DELLA FRANCESCA

SKIRA

Title Page: Angel's Head, detail from the Virgin and Child with Saints
and Angels. Pinacoteca di Brera, Milan.

★

★

Distributed in the United States by
THE WORLD PUBLISHING COMPANY
2231 West 110th Street, Cleveland 2, Ohio

PIERO DELLA FRANCESCA

of all Italian painters, is the one to whom our modern sensibility most readily responds. In the Church of San Francesco at Arezzo and in the museums where they hang, his paintings cast a spell on the visitor; they initiate him into a spiritual realm in which men and women like ourselves walk in the sunlight of eternity. The trend towards abstraction that has transformed art since the beginning of the 20th century finds a noble precedent in Piero della Francesca's taste for contemplation, which he always gratified at the expense of action. Reality and abstraction, humanity and contemplation—these are the ingredients of his art; each holds its own and harmonizes with the others. Master of serene colors, adept in geometry and mathematics, creator of monumental forms, Piero della Francesca stands out, between Masaccio and Leonardo, as one of the great spokesmen of Renaissance humanism.

PIERO DELLA FRANCESCA

PROPHET, DETAIL. THE STORY OF THE TRUE CROSS.
FRESCO, CHURCH OF SAN FRANCESCO, AREZZO.

PIERO DELLA FRANCESCA'S IDEAL OF LIFE

Each time we come away from Piero della Francesca's work as a whole, we are left with a feeling of soaring grandeur and monumentality. But as artists of many periods and places have achieved some form of monumental expression, what, we may ask ourselves, is so particular about Piero's? First of all there is his equanimity. Undemonstrative, or indifferent to emotion, he neither loves nor hates, nor even smiles or weeps. Where Masaccio brings towering moral forces into play, forces captained by a God made man, whose miracle-working disciples impose His rule on earth, Piero's art is a monument of contemplative beauty. In it life goes imperturbably on as if time had never been; in it, indeed, life and death seem to merge into another sphere of existence transcending them both.

Not that Piero is devoid of a moral sense. But he never displays it by an action completed, nor even by an act of faith. His moral integrity is inherent in his artistry, every picture, every figure bespeaking grave, impassible, majestic dignity. Instead of pictures of God on earth, he gives us those of an extra-historical race created without the distinctions class and place give rise to—fabulous men arisen momentarily out of the mists of time, epic heroes of a saga painted instead of written.

Piero's mode of expression differs from that which springs from action and faith by its ingenuousness. He attains to the epic with such ease and spontaneity, avoiding any hint of artifice or strain, that his poetry may properly be termed "naïve"; it is as innocent as the almond blossom. Compared with Masaccio's Olympian driving power, as he reincarnates divine beings on an earthly plane, Piero's poetry is almost that of the people, nearer as it is to man taken in a generalized, popular sense. In him we find that popular, that childish delight in luxurious, Oriental garments, fantastic headdress, and the arms and armor of knightly tournaments. In fact, when the Council of Florence convened in 1439, with its processions and pageantry, Piero must have seen with his own eyes much of what he painted in the frescos in the Church of San Francesco at Arezzo, particularly the scenes of the battle of Constantine and the reception of the Queen of Sheba.

Yet, the very way he goes about a picture suggests that Piero consciously countered ostentation with the best of all correctives: a keen sense of irony. The Queen of Sheba's ladies in waiting, the grooms tending the horses, the envoys come to restore the True Cross—all of them savor of it. His irony brings home to us the detachment with which he handled his subjects, and wonderfully tempers the geometric abstraction of his forms. Irony and abstraction blended are, we may say, the filter through which he passes the data of reality. He succeeds in doing so because, at the same time, he actually has a powerful streak of realism in him, and gets it across by means of a formal abstraction that is nothing else but a subtle way of symbolizing irony.

But he also attaches another meaning to his abstract approach to form. For he subscribed to the cult of man, to the confident faith in human capacities that Renaissance culture spoke for, when it placed man *a priori* in the center of the universe. This ideal Masaccio expressed in the purity and power of his art. Piero nourished much the same ideal, yet not quite the same, his being somewhat more far-reaching, more finely shaded. With its lusty vigor of form, a picture by Masaccio concomitantly creates the space in which it is contained; whereas Piero's space, though also enveloping the depiction of men and things, has a strictly pictorial value of its own, whose ineluctable effect is to transmit the monumental aura of the figures—i.e. of man—to everything that surrounds them. Not so highly concentrated as Masaccio's, Piero's monumentality embraces the world and broadcasts its humanizing influence. With one foot in eternity, his men and women have a right to stand as they do, utterly calm. The potential vitality of his architecture is due to the fact that it, too, shares in the intellectual abstraction in which his figures are clothed. Hence a refreshing fusing and interpenetration, figures becoming architectural and architecture humanized.

The ideal of life that shines through his work is best understood in the light of humanist ideas in general. Both Coluccio Salutati and Leonardo Bruni stressed the moral and religious vigor of the humanist outlook as against the aloofness of the Stoics from the social order. "What counts," writes E. Garin in *L'Umanesimo italiano* (1952, page 58), "is not the static meditation of the recluse, not Aristotelian theorizing, Stoic asceticism, or the monastic life. Men are meant to live in charitable concert with one another. And though Bruni's way of putting the problem very much savors of Aristotle, and of Aristotelian ethics, the spirit behind it all is thoroughly Christian. His is a Christianity deliberately setting up against the Greek ideal of contemplation a more active principle, aimed at promoting the general welfare." Imbued as he was with the contemplative spirit, Piero was obviously out of step with the nascent Italian humanism of his time, as Bruni pictures it. Masaccio, on the other hand, was wholly at one with it.

As we move on from Bruni (1370-1444) to Leon Battista Alberti (1404-1472), we feel that a change has crept over men's outlook on life. And though an outlook no less moral in tenor, "Fate" had now given way to "Virtue"—virtue in the sense of loving-kindness, moral soundness, a "saintly discipline of living." But Alberti does not keep to a purely moral sphere. In Cristoforo Landino's *Disputationes Camaldulenses*, he is made the champion of contemplative values in art, as against Lorenzo de' Medici, who held the good of art to consist in the sense of security and comfort it gives the people. When Alberti lifts up his mind's eye, he finds God in the beauty of things, not in their utility. He thus considerably broadens the scope of the moral life as Bruni had conceived it. For him the active life is quite compatible with the contemplative aspirations that give man knowledge of God. In the community and in the bosom of the family is to be found the basis of the moral life; even art is based on the knowledge of man and not on an emanation from God, as Plotinus believed—though art, by its very nature, transcends the earthly and human, and attains to the knowledge of God, or to some measure of it.

Less rigorous, less intense than the older ideal, Alberti's is satisfyingly vast and all-embracing, reconciling contemplation with action and corresponding perfectly to the ideal world of Piero della Francesca.

THE EYE OF THE MIND

If ever there was a time when creative art went hand in hand with scientific research, this was at Florence in the 15th century. Painting as a representational art then meant, first of all, painting as a means of learning more about man and the natural world, and the relationship between the two. Because they put it on an equal footing with science the Florentines of the Quattrocento set painting free of the humble, craftsmanly traditions of the Middle Ages. It did not occur to them that there might be other spheres of knowledge beyond that of science, but luckily for art they made no attempt to keep within strictly logical, mathematical limits. We may say, on the contrary, that they let themselves go, exulting in the newly won freedom of their creative imagination and wisely regarding strict processes of thought as no more than a distant conclusion, a working definition of an end in view.

Piero della Francesca wrote two treatises, one on perspective, the other on the five regular bodies, both treated from a purely mathematical angle, i.e. disregarding everything that takes its rise in the psycho-physical world. Here is how he defined his art: "Painting is nothing else but a demonstration of planes and solids made smaller or greater according to their term." (By "term" he meant the distance at which they are seen.) This, we should remember, is a definition made by an old man at the far end of his career, as he pored over the experiences of a lifetime, hoping to pass them on to artists to come. His pictures themselves, needless to say, are in no sense the application of pre-established rules, but obey laws unknown even to the artist, laws he unwittingly laid down as he worked onward.

When in the early 15th century Brunelleschi presented painters with the rules of perspective—worked out mathematically, but not yet tested empirically—, he implicitly gave them at the same time the notion of homogeneous space, existing quite apart from the material world.

In his treatise on painting written in 1435 and dedicated to Brunelleschi, Leon Battista Alberti set perspective the task of carrying painting back to its one great source: nature herself. Knowledge of the real world, then, was not to be ascertained from the divine revelations in which the Middle Ages put its faith, but from a systematic study of nature's laws, among them those of perspective.

Keen-minded geometer that he was, Piero studied perspective with somewhat more rigor than Alberti did. He wrote scientifically on perspective and regular bodies, but did not bother his head about theorizing on other aspects of painting.

For him his writings were a theoretical summing-up of his experience—i.e. the lifelong experience of a painter practicing his craft—which, for the most part, had consisted of efforts and aspirations that in themselves had nothing to do with perspective. It would be a mistake to think that Piero came to paint as he did for mathematical reasons. It is none the less true that his ideal of life as we have attempted to define it—which, of course, was also a way of thinking and feeling—tallied surprisingly well with his conceptions of perspective and geometry.

In any number of his paintings we find that each figure and object aspires to the state of a geometrical form. I say "aspires" advisedly, for aspiration is the secret of his art. The vitality of his pictures is sustained precisely because, for Piero, pure geometry was a goal he took good care not to reach. Take the tree and the second angel in the London *Baptism*; both of them long to become cylinders or columns, and both of them accordingly assume an enigmatic stateliness. Yet they remain very much a tree and an angel, their presence made even realer, more physical by their well-rounded geometrical solidity.

Plato regarded absolute beauty as existing solely in geometrical forms. Piero evidently agreed, and the beauty of the Queen of Sheba's retinue in the Arezzo frescos is largely due to an almost cylindrical roundness of form. Even the beauty of the walled hill-town in the background of *The Finding of the Cross* cannot be said to stem from the perspective in which we see it, for the houses are built up flatly, vertically, in the mediaeval fashion; rather it is the all but abstract simplicity of the forms of the houses, together with the impinging light, that creates all their poetry. So it is, again, with the two landscapes on the back of the Uffizi portraits of Federigo da Montefeltro and Battista Sforza; the spell they cast issues from the ponderous rhythm of the broad-based cones formed by the hills beyond.

The yearning for geometrical regularity is stronger in Piero's work than in that of any other Quattrocento artist; it is, in fact, the corollary of his ideal of monumental structure.

Perspective defines the picture-space in which the human figures are to live and move. The latter may, if a painter pleases, loom so large as to be out of all proportion with the picture-space, as is the case with Masaccio's figures in the Brancacci Chapel. And though still indispensable, perspective thus plays a distinctly secondary role, completely overshadowed by the human element.

Piero's feeling for perspective was too keen for him not to keep it well in the forefront. Yet how significant it is that, with a single exception, to be dealt with in a moment, the human element in his pictures is never swallowed up in space. Each scene is invariably laid out in front of the space created by means of perspective, never within it; or else an impression of perspective is set up amidst the figures of a group or crowd, very often in order to lend them consistency and fullness, but never is it communicated to the things that surround them. This may seem like an odd procedure for one so enamored of perspective as Piero was, but the reason for it will readily be made clear by a few examples.

Let us begin with the exception referred to above: the left half of the Urbino *Flagellation*. What we have here is a kind of tunnel in which perspective is applied to the hilt, with such care that the illusion of space is complete. That no hint of monumentality remains is due precisely to the "hole" in which the figures are inserted. Their attitudes are wonderfully graceful and stately; that of the man wielding the whip is worthy of some antique statue of an outstretched hero. But if we are to get the slightest flavor of monumentality out of these figures, they have to be imagined without the architecture, or seen as a detail in photographic reproduction, lifted from their context.

Not only monumental, but among Piero's finest figure paintings are the bystanders in the right foreground of this picture. Their grandeur, furthermore, is not simply a matter of form and stance, but also partakes of the deep, kaleidoscopic recession beside them, on the left. At moments like this we realize what perspective meant to Piero; it was a form of pure beauty of which he availed himself with full creative license. This picture comes down to two distinct scenes: one is all space and receding perspective (so much so that the actual scene of Christ scourged becomes merely incidental), the other is a group of three motionless figures. Artistically speaking, no line can be drawn between the two scenes, for they blend into an organic whole. After this we need not be surprised to find three pictures (at Urbino, Berlin and Baltimore) by disciples of his in which nothing more than houses seen in perspective are shown. This is characteristic of Piero, and a trait no other Quattrocento artist shares with him.

But *The Flagellation* is an exceptional example of his way of linking up perspective and figures. More typical is *The Queen of Sheba's Visit to King Solomon*. As must soon be noticed in studying his work, Piero's habitual point of view is fairly low-lying, with the result that "the lower part of bodies becomes disproportionately long and takes on a dignified sturdiness. This angle of vision also accounts for his habit of distributing figures densely along the lower half of the picture, thus laying stress on the over-all constructive solidity, while distances between everything lying at the top of the picture are cut short" (Nicco Fasola in a note, page 51, to his edition of Piero della Francesca's *De Prospectiva Pingendi*). In other words, perspective thrusts space far back into the picture, leaving the foreground free for human figures. This we see clearly enough in the right half of the fresco, where the room containing the figures might have been expected to swallow them up. But nothing of the sort happens. On the contrary, the colonnaded chamber sets off the figures, which appear to be in the foreground, as if none of the space around them existed. The Corinthian column, rather than defining the picture-space, as might be supposed, actually serves to divide the scene neatly in two, like an initial signpost preceding even the immediate foreground.

In *The Resurrection* at Borgo San Sepolcro Piero also took good care not to push perspective too far. And while the stone sarcophagus, the four slumbering soldiers and Christ's upraised leg form a unified whole, seen in perspective, Christ's long-suffering face floats to the picture-surface out of the sky behind, casting a spell that is almost thaumaturgical.

That perspective plays a key part in this art no one can deny, but some have certainly stretched the point. Piero kept his geometry well in hand, guiding it to the ends he intended it for, never guided by it. Late in life he came to paint several works in application of his theories. These are not his best works, however, nor do the qualities they have in any way hinge on the ideas behind them.

What we may note here is the symbolical side of Piero's use of geometry. Simply modeling figures after geometrical forms is not enough to put across movement and action. So great are Masaccio's dramatic tension and formal energy that they suggest potential action even when figures stand quite still. But tension is out of keeping with the ideals of geometry. Thus it is that Piero stopped short at contemplation, forsaking action. The contemplative spirit feeds on symbols. And though, as far as innovations of form and perspective are concerned, a whole cultural age stands between Piero's *Virgin Annunciate* and a Byzantine *Virgin* (those at Torcello and Murano, for example), yet their contemplative serenity is the same. Each, instead of representing action, presents a scene. If we think for a moment what the real trends of late Quattrocento art were, we realize that Antonio Pollaiolo and Leonardo were the leaders of taste, the heralds of the art to come, and not Piero. But what we must also realize is that Piero reconciled an almost scientific precision with a full measure of creative freedom, by the same token achieving a perfection of form that embraced both the symbolic vision of the Middle Ages and the objectivity of modern times.

THE EYE OF THE SENSES

"We may be certain," writes Roberto Longhi (*Piero della Francesca*, page 47), "that our initial impression of the Arezzo frescos will be overwhelmingly one of color. I never revisit the Church of San Francesco without experiencing the same uprush of feeling that came over me the first time I stood before that 'sacred wall,' with its greens and pinks, browns and whites, as fresh and pure as open meadowlands, a babe's cheek or limpid springwater... These are the colors of the world at the first dawn of time, as the sun broke over the earth."

Piero sees color with the eye of his senses. He approaches and discovers the world by way of color. Scientifically applied perspective and ideals of form, whether monumental or geometrical, came afterwards. For him color is neither more nor less than a primeval state of things, the foil of his naïveté, the logos of creative spontaneity; it is, in the last analysis, the cornerstone of his greatness as an artist. But however spontaneous and agreeably naïve it may strike us at first sight, it cannot be dismissed so lightly, but must be reckoned for what it is: a highly complex quantity.

The art circles in which young Piero moved at Borgo and Arezzo were predominantly Sienese—in other words, thoroughly versed in the handling of color, though still ignorant of the latest changes wrought on form by the Florentines. As luck would have it, Piero went to Florence, where he must have studied Masaccio and soon come abreast of the most advanced art developments of his day. In 1439 he is known to have been at Florence in the bottega of Domenico Veneziano, a Venetian who had wisely come to Tuscany at an opportune moment, and a master brought up—as far as color is concerned—in the traditions of the Late Gothic school, as were also the Sienese, be it remembered.

The Gothic use of color, even in its final phase, was based on harmonies of various shades of red, green and blue. Not that it was entirely lacking in finely shaded plays of light and shadow, but these were confined to local tones. This is to say that a composition was invariably organized in terms of lines or forms, or both, and not of chiaroscuro. Not even the 15th-century Flemish masters, whose use of local tones was much more refined than that of the Tuscans, ever dreamt of composing in terms of light and shade. This had to wait for the coming of the great 16th-century Venetians.

All the same, color as we find it in Florentine painting of the first half of the 15th century is highly subtle and intricate, thanks largely to a knowledge of form-entwining chiaroscuro far in advance of Gothic traditions.

What exactly Masaccio's conception of color was is hard to say. He was the first to model form in chiaroscuro, a procedure that lies at the origin of all 15th-century Florentine painting. But the frescos in the Brancacci Chapel are too poorly preserved for us to tell whether he really made the most of chiaroscuro, getting from it the full effects it implies. We certainly find surprising plays of light around the Christchild's head in his *Virgin and Child* at the National Gallery, London. But this is slender evidence, far too meager for us to assume that such practices were usual with Masaccio.

As for Domenico Veneziano—who, before settling at Florence, was very probably shaped by Late Northern Gothic traditions, along the lines we find in Pisanello—he brought the Florentines the full fruit of his experience in capitalizing on local tones. In him we find the origin of Piero's light and shadow. His is a light that takes on all the semblance of real light, played off as it is in distinct tracts against equally distinct tracts of shadow, to the intensification of each. Both Domenico and Piero in fact, instead of shading a single color by means of chiaroscuro, call on one color for light and another for shadow. Obviously, even if conceived in terms of color, chiaroscuro will always retain its original character: a contrast of black and white, which are not colors. And though the interwoven patterns of light and shadow are far richer and more highly developed in Piero than in Domenico, at bottom there is no difference between them on this score.

But Domenico Veneziano's color and Masaccio's chiaroscuro do not sufficiently account for Piero's light-and-shade. There is an intense light potential in Piero's pigment; it is everywhere stressed, and from it runs a fine scale of shadings that culminate in shadow. It is not too much to say that Piero fully possessed the secret of color-light, which he probably inherited directly from Fra Angelico. The all-pervading "color of paradise" we so often find in the latter's altar-pictures became pure color-light in Piero's hands.

Roberto Longhi calls it actual daylight, that indeed of high noon. But Focillon rightly observes that, cool and immutable as it is, there is no fixing an hour for light like this. I would go farther. Neither Piero's light nor his color are of this world; they are visitants from legend, or from undiscovered sidereal regions where white glistens with a tonic power, where pinks and blues hint at the unspeakable tenderness with which light caresses earthly things.

Piero never set out to paint an historical scene in the actual light of day. What he did, by and large, was to make his color the vehicle of a delicate or tender expression of feeling, and this is what gives their entire conviction to the stately-solemn gravity of his forms.

Piero's keen feeling for color-light had an inevitable impact on his conception of form. To convince ourselves of this, we need only compare the magnificent nude in the foreground of *The Death of Adam* at Arezzo, its easy, natural pose and thickset, sensuous body, with the frailer (and more anatomically correct) body of Christ standing in the Jordan, in the London *Baptism*. When Corot first exhibited a nude, Ingres' pupils were quick to observe that his was a landscapist's conception of the nude. The same might be said of Piero, who, with his extreme, poetic sensitiveness to color and light, seems to hew his nudes out of the atmospheric light in which they stand, instead of building them up, systematically, in terms of their anatomical structure. No need to dwell on the contrast between them and Pollaiolo's "anatomical" nudes.

Another outcome of his feeling for color is his predilection for heraldry. The profiles of the Queen of Sheba, Battista Sforza, Federigo da Montefeltro, and Sigismondo Malatesta and his two dogs, one white, the other black, together with a profusion of staffs, lances, halberds, banners, horses' legs and so on—all are tokens of the delight he took in emblazoning the picture with heraldic devices.

Also stemming from his fine flair for color is his use of rhythmic breaks in composition. Even when the scene forms an organic whole and the picture-space calls for no particular breaking up, even then he will cut off one element or figure from another and divide the surface into two distinct zones. This practice, too, is part and parcel of mediaeval tradition, when such divisions were necessary to the narrative. Piero clung to it, though he usually managed withal to sacrifice nothing of his spatial unity, e.g. *Heraclius restoring the Cross to Jerusalem*, or *The Victory of Constantine over Maxentius*, nominally a battle scene, though the two emperors and their respective armies are quite distinct from each other, linked only by the small white cross in the center. An exception is *The Victory of Heraclius over Chosroes*, which, for all its good points, makes too great concessions to the subject itself.

Piero's love of color it is, in any event, that prompts him not to concentrate on the human figure alone, but to impress his deep feeling for all that is vital and human on the full and empty spaces of the picture alike, on architecture as well as figures, on the heavens he paints as well as the earth.

HIS LIFE

No reliable account of the artist's life has come down to us, so that to get some idea of the man and his career we are more or less obliged to feel our way. Though held in esteem by his contemporaries, and an occasional guest at the brilliant courts of Ferrara, Rimini, Urbino and Rome, Piero della Francesca seems to have been appreciated more as a technician, adept in matters of perspective and geometry, than as a painter. He came to Florence at a peak period in the city's temporal and artistic greatness; but then a young and little known pupil of Domenico Veneziano, he attracted no attention. Most of his life was quietly spent at his native Borgo San Sepolcro and at nearby Arezzo.

He was obviously a slow and meticulous worker. His polyptych of the Misericordia, ordered in 1445, was not finished until shortly before 1462. And when they commissioned an altarpiece from him in 1454, the friars of Sant'Agostino at Borgo—apparently familiar with his ways—granted him eight years for the work. He was to need almost twice as much time, not finishing the picture until 1469. Since he is known to have employed several assistants, we may assume his extreme slowness to be intimately connected with his character, and with the cool detachment of a keenly critical mind.

Quite willing, apparently, to bear his share of civic duties, he was elected to the Town Council at Borgo San Sepolcro, where he lived more or less withdrawn from the world at large. Though this enabled him to paint as he pleased, it doomed him to a certain obscurity; his reputation is much higher today than it ever was in his own time.

In reconstituting Piero's life and career, we have nothing more definite to go on than the following notices, culled for the most part from old records.

1410-1420. Birth at Borgo San Sepolcro, probably between these two dates, of Piero, son of Benedetto de' Franceschi and Romana di Perino da Monterchi. Why he came to be called *della* Francesca instead of *dei* Franceschi is not known. But since records dating from 1462 refer to him as *della Francesca*, this form of the name, which seems to have gained currency in his lifetime, is the one tacitly agreed on by critics today.

1439 (September 7). First mention of Pietro di Benedetto dal Borgo, as an assistant in the workshop of Domenico Veneziano at Florence while the latter was painting some frescos in the choir of Sant'Egidio.

1442. Elected Town Councilor at Borgo San Sepolcro.

1445 (January 11). The Compagnia della Misericordia at Borgo commissioned an altarpiece from Piero, to be delivered in three years' time. This is taken to be the polyptych now in the Palazzo Comunale at Borgo. The contract stipulated that it should be the work of his own hands, carried out without assistants. In 1462 the Compagnia settled up with Marco di Benedetto, paying him for "the picture painted by Messer Pietro, his brother." We may assume this to be the same polyptych.

1448-1450. Probable time of a stay at Ferrara, where he painted a fresco in the Palace, mentioned by Vasari but no longer extant. This is borne out not only by strains of his art discernible in Ferrarese painting, but also by very obvious imitations of his style in local manuscripts, e.g. the Bible of Borso d'Este in the Biblioteca Estense at Modena, containing miniatures painted between 1455 and 1461, and other manuscripts in the library at Cesena, which was founded between 1447 and 1450. (See Mario Salmi's article on *La Bibbia di Borso d'Este e Piero della Francesca*, in *La Rinascita*, July-September 1943, page 365).

1451. In this year Piero signed his great fresco in the Tempio Malatestiano at Rimini, which shows Sigismondo Pandolfo Malatesta kneeling before St Sigismund.

1454 (October 4). Commissioned to paint an altarpiece for the Church of Sant'Agostino at Borgo, to be delivered in eight years' time. On November 14, 1469, a payment was made for this work, which he had presumably just completed.

1459 (April 12). Piero was working in Rome and received payment "for his part in the painting of several pictures in the chamber of His Holiness the Pope." No trace of this work remains, nor any other reference to it.

1466 (December 20). Commissioned by the Compagnia dell'Annunziata at Arezzo to paint a gonfalon celebrating the Annunciation. This work too has been lost.

1466. In the records of the Compagnia dell'Annunziata, it is also stated that Piero "painted the main dome (*chupola*) in the Church of San Francesco at Arezzo." Now *chupola* is an obvious error for *chapela*. We may take it then that by 1466 the painting in the main chapel of San Francesco was finished. This is the only date relating to these frescos that we can fix with certainty. It is known that the Bacci family first commissioned Bicci di Lorenzo to decorate the chapel in 1447; but Bicci died in 1452 after finishing the vault, so that Piero must have painted the chapel in his stead sometime between 1452 and 1466. As no other interpretation of the known facts is plausible, no other assumption as to the dating of this work is worth considering. The most we can add is that the painting may have been interrupted for a time while Piero carried out the work in Rome, now lost, referred to above.

1466. In 1466 Ferabò, the humanist from Verona, made a point of reminding Federigo da Montefeltro of the portrait of him painted by Piero della Francesca. And since Ferabò was at Urbino in 1465, the work presumably dates from that same year or earlier. We cannot reasonably assume this to be the same portrait as the one now in the Uffizi, which forms a diptych with that of Battista Sforza, who died at the age of twenty-six in 1472. Some Latin verses inscribed on the diptych speak of her in the past tense; so this work must have been painted after her death, i.e. after 1472.

In 1469 Piero was staying at Urbino with Giovanni Santi, Raphael's father; he had come to discuss the terms of a picture, but which one exactly it is now impossible to tell.

Sometime after 1482 he dedicated his treatise *De Quinque Corporibus Regularibus* to Guidobaldo da Montefeltro, reminding the Duke that to his father, Federigo, he had given the best of himself unstintingly, and that now, at the time of writing the dedication, he felt very old indeed.

Two works painted at Urbino are extant: *The Flagellation* and the altar-picture in the Brera at Milan, originally in the Church of San Bernardino at Urbino. If he produced them no more rapidly than his other works, he must have stayed for a considerable time at Urbino. With no more than stylistic evidence to go on, it is no easy matter deducing their dates, and this must remain largely guesswork. However, it is reasonable to suppose that *The Flagellation* antedates the Arezzo frescos, while the altar-picture in the Brera would seem to number among his last works. It was certainly at Urbino, too, that Piero gave lessons in perspective to no less a pupil than Bramante, as related by Sabba da Castiglione in 1549.

1467. Piero was at Borgo San Sepolcro, holding an official post as Town Councilor.

1468. Fleeing the plague, Piero took refuge at Bastia, near Perugia, where he finished the gonfalon for Arezzo commissioned in 1466. On November 7 the work was taken possession of by the cardinal camerlingo of the Compagnia dell'Annunziata and conveyed in an open cart to Arezzo, where it was "found beautiful and highly praised."

1469. Received a payment at Borgo San Sepolcro for his Sant'Agostino altarpiece, commissioned fifteen years before.

1471. Cited for failure to pay his taxes.

1474. Received payment for the frescos in the Chapel of the Madonna at the Abbey Church, Borgo, now lost.

1478. Painted a fresco of the Virgin, now lost, for the Compagnia della Misericordia at Borgo San Sepolcro.

1480-1482. Head of the Priors of the Confraternità di San Bartolomeo at Borgo San Sepolcro.

1482. Rented a comfortable house at Rimini, where he had work to carry out. Sometime after 1482 Piero dedicated his treatises on mathematics and perspective to Guidobaldo da Montefeltro, Duke of Urbino.

1487. Made his will at Borgo San Sepolcro, "sound in mind and body." Written partly in his own hand, this will proves that he was not yet blind.

1492 (October 1). Buried in the *Badia* at Borgo San Sepolcro. According to Vasari, he had gone blind in his last years and was led by the hand by one Marco di Longaro.

HIS WORKS

I

POLYPTYCH OF THE MISERICORDIA

THE BAPTISM OF CHRIST

ST JEROME AND A DONOR, GIROLAMO AMADI

ST SIGISMUND WORSHIPPED BY SIGISMONDO PANDOLFO MALATESTA

THE FLAGELLATION

POLYPTYCH OF THE MISERICORDIA

Palazzo Comunale, Borgo San Sepolcro

THIS altarpiece is the first work known to have been commissioned from Piero della Francesca. The gold background, in keeping with a mediaeval tradition that still lingered on, was a condition imposed on him by the churchmen who ordered the picture. Hence the glaring contrast between the strongly modeled forms and the uniform gold background, which, with its gleaming plays of reflected light, is inimical to sculptural form. This anomaly is impressed upon us not only in various parts and details of the polyptych, but above all in the central panel, known as the *Madonna della Misericordia*. Here, formed by the ample folds of the Virgin's outspread mantle, and sharply contrasting with the gold background, a whole tent-like area of space is created in which the congregated faithful humbly kneel, with uplifted eyes. The frontal position of the Virgin and her hieratic erectness are characteristic remnants of the Middle Ages. But her sculptural form is a sign of new times, and spells the Renaissance.

Significant for the way in which form is built up, and for its novel solution of the problem of space, this work looks both to the future and the past, and achieves a fruitful synthesis that only Piero can make us accept: one of form and color, of assertive vigor and placidity veiled in contemplation, of both Renaissance and mediaeval ideals.

Forming the upper panel of the polyptych, *The Crucifixion* is certainly the most poignant scene Piero ever painted; nothing so emotional in tenor was ever to appear in his work again.

◀ THE MADONNA OF MERCY, DETAIL. CENTRAL PANEL OF THE POLYPTYCH OF THE MISERICORDIA, PALAZZO COMUNALE, BORGO SAN SEPOLCRO.

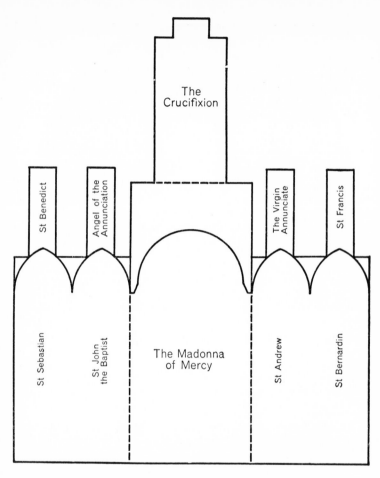

The
Crucifixion

St Benedict

Angel of the
Annunciation

The Virgin
Annunciate

St Francis

St Sebastian

St John
the Baptist

The Madonna
of Mercy

St Andrew

St Bernardin

PLAN OF THE POLYPTYCH OF THE MISERICORDIA.
PALAZZO COMUNALE, BORGO SAN SEPOLCRO.

THE MADONNA OF MERCY. CENTRAL PANEL OF THE POLYPTYCH ▶
OF THE MISERICORDIA, PALAZZO COMUNALE, BORGO SAN SEPOLCRO.

It is a masterpiece that, even if it alone remained, would still make him the only immediate heir worthy of Masaccio, whose great *Crucifixion*, painted in 1426 for the Church of the Carmine at Pisa, had already set a standard never to be surpassed.

Piero's polyptych was contracted for by the Compagnia della Misericordia at Borgo San Sepolcro on January 11, 1445, delivery being stipulated in three years' time (these records were published by Milanesi in *Il Buonarroti*, page 116, in 1885). But it must have been completed only many years afterwards, if we may judge from a part-payment for it made to the artist's brother Marco in 1462 (Gronau covers this point in *Repertorium für Kunstwissenschaft*, 1900, page 393).

One or two other points provide us with cross-references to the dating, namely the fact that the two saints pictured here —St Andrew and St Bernardin—must have been painted after 1450, the year in which the latter was canonized. There is also the fact that the predella and the small figures of saints on either side are undoubtedly the work of an assistant, whom Mario Salmi (in *La Rivista d'Arte*, XXIV, 1942, pp. 26-44) surmises to be the painter and illuminator Giuliano Amedei.

Vasari mentions this altarpiece, but for some reason wrongly refers to it as a fresco. When the Compagnia della Misericordia was disbanded in 1807, the polyptych was dismantled. Subsequently scattered, the panels were reassembled somewhat later —in 1892, as a matter of fact, in commemoration of the four hundredth anniversary of the artist's death (see *Arte e Storia*, 1892, page 232). They were then placed in the Church of San Rocco, at Borgo San Sepolcro, new seat of the Brotherhood.

The work on the whole has come down to us in a very poor state of preservation.

◄ THE CRUCIFIXION. UPPER PANEL OF THE POLYPTYCH OF THE MISERICORDIA, PALAZZO COMUNALE, BORGO SAN SEPOLCRO.

THE BAPTISM OF CHRIST
National Gallery, London

W E HAVE no external evidence to go on in dating this painting, but everything points to its being a youthful work.
Landscape is an intimate feature of Piero's art, which counts on
it for an element of garden-like freshness. The whole scene here
is one of subdued incantation, of placid cheer, of naïve confidence
in the future of the world, in eternal youth and perennial spring;
the angels and tree betoken beauty, Christ and St John human
dignity, nakedness chastity. Piero has never heard of original
sin. So strong indeed is the impression of spontaneity that we
feel he improvised his color-scheme as he went along. Juxtaposed
tracts of color sustain and counterbalance zones of light and
shadow—a tenuous, otherworldly light, rendered doubly pure
by hues whose delicacy borders on the intangible.

First heard of in the Priory of San Giovanni Battista at Borgo
San Sepolcro, this painting was removed to the Cathedral in 1808
when the Priory was secularized. In 1859 it was purchased from
the Bishop and Chapter by Sir J. C. Robinson on behalf of
Matthew Uzielli of London. At the Uzielli sale in 1861 it was
acquired by the National Gallery.

No records relating to *The Baptism* are known to exist. There
are good reasons for believing, however, that it originally
formed part of a triptych, whose side panels, attributed to Matteo
di Giovanni, are grotesquely discordant, both as to style and
scale, with Piero's picture.

The present condition of this work is remarkably good.

THE BAPTISM OF CHRIST. $(66 \times 45\frac{3}{4}'')$ BY COURTESY OF THE TRUSTEES, ▶
NATIONAL GALLERY, LONDON.

PAGE 38: IDEM, DETAIL OF THE ANGELS.
PAGE 39: IDEM, DETAIL OF THE LANDSCAPE.

ST JEROME AND A DONOR, GIROLAMO AMADI. (19¼ × 16½″)
GALLERIA DELL'ACCADEMIA, VENICE.

ST JEROME AND A DONOR, GIROLAMO AMADI

Galleria dell'Accademia, Venice

THIS painting, too, has all the earmarks of a youthful work. Its style on the whole, however, seems more mature than that of *The Baptism*. The landscape is a vast open stretch of space typical of Piero, while the tree on the right stands in the ground with all the sturdy conviction of nature herself. The slight, well-knit figure of St Jerome is so placed as to convey the impression that he is about to turn still further sideways; but this is a clever, discreet and quite successful device for integrating him into the picture-space.

The figure of Amadi, it must be admitted, betrays a hand still a little unsure of itself. Piero seems to have been unable to get the balance he wanted between the sharply isolated profile of the donor and the receding vista of space and mountainous country behind. In fact the picture may well have been originally planned without him.

Nothing is known of Girolamo Amadi, though pictures by a well-to-do namesake of his, a Venetian, were commissioned from Nicolò di Pietro and Gentile da Fabriano in 1408. We are thus entitled to surmise that, very possibly, this picture was painted for a Venetian donor with whom Piero had come in contact, but where or how we cannot say.

The work bears two inscriptions. On the treetrunk to the left: PETRI DE BVRGO SANCTI SEPVLCRI OPVS. And beneath the donor: HIER. AMADI. AVG. F.

The picture first came to light when it entered the Gallery of the Academy in 1850 with the Hellman-Renier bequest.

ST SIGISMUND WORSHIPPED BY SIGISMONDO PANDOLFO MALATESTA

Tempio Malatestiano, Rimini

THIS fresco, bearing the date of 1451, shows Piero in what may be called his "heraldic style." The whole tone of the work is set by the two hounds, one black, one white, with their juxtaposed profiles; the absence of perspective, the architecture flattened out on the picture-surface, and the patterned festoons serve to confirm the artist's stylistic intentions. Like St Jerome in the small picture at Venice, St Sigismund is viewed slightly sidewise, in order to fit him solidly into the space his patriarchal figure needs to contain it. But the razor-sharp profile of Malatesta betrays no inkling of the unsteadiness we scented in that of Girolamo Amadi; on the contrary, both spiritually and visually, his figure is the focal point of the composition.

The court of the Malatestas at Rimini, we may well imagine, impressed Piero both by its magnificence and its genuinely aristocratic character. Its tastes and manners were still those of the Late Middle Ages, until suddenly, with Leon Battista Alberti and Piero della Francesca, it found itself in the vanguard of Renaissance innovations. We see this everywhere in the Tempio Malatestiano, with its grafting on of the "divine proportions" to Gothic eccentricities.

The heraldic style of Piero's fresco, remnant of the Middle Ages that it is, here joins on to the very strain of Renaissance finesse and elegance called for to mellow its formalism.

ST SIGISMUND WORSHIPPED BY SIGISMONDO PANDOLFO MALATESTA.
FRESCO DATED 1451. TEMPIO MALATESTIANO, RIMINI.
PAGE 42: DETAIL OF ST SIGISMUND, LEFT SIDE.
PAGE 44: DETAIL OF SIGISMONDO MALATESTA, CENTER.

An inscription reads as follows: SANCTVS SIGISMVNDVS. SIGISMVNDVS PANDVLFVS MALATESTA PAN. F. PETRI DE BVRGO OPVS MCCCCLI. Though partially obliterated now, this date is reasonably certain, as it refers to the decoration of the Temple. Commemorating the building of Sigismondo's Castle, a second inscription runs: CASTELLVMSISM VNDVM ARIMINENSE MCCCCXLVI.

ST SIGISMUND WORSHIPPED BY SIGISMONDO PANDOLFO MALATESTA.
FRESCO DATED 1451. TEMPIO MALATESTIANO, RIMINI.

THE FLAGELLATION
Galleria Nazionale delle Marche, Urbino

A MARVEL of synthesis, this work gives us all the threads of Piero's style, crystallized in its ideal state. Perspective and color-light have become one and indivisible; the tones of the foreground figures, that is, blend so well into the architecture behind that the latter becomes a source of light. These three figures are men of flesh and blood, and one is wearing a costly robe of velvet, with rich, brocaded patterns. But the perspective burrows deep into the background beside them, and there is a slow stirring of memory before we can center our attention on the Scourging of Christ, so far away in time. All this poetry issues from the remembering mind, as it lingers over a bygone martyrdom still miraculously real enough to convey a powerful human presence. Poetry and allegory here become one.

Local tradition identifies the persons shown as Oddantonio da Montefeltro, Count of Urbino, flanked by the two advisors insidiously provided him by Sigismondo Malatesta. These men, Manfredo de' Pii di Cesena and Tommaso di Guido dell'Agnello, proved in fact to be the undoing of Oddantonio, who was finally murdered in 1444. His step-brother, Federigo da Montefeltro, who then took power, was strongly suspected of having had a hand in the plot. To soothe his conscience, Federigo may well have commissioned this picture as a votive offering to the memory of Oddantonio, made the paragon of no less a person than Christ and shown suffering at the hands of his two traitorous advisors, his scourgers.

Though all this smacks very much of the popular imagination, it may well be the actual explanation of the scene.

Sir Kenneth Clark has quite rightly objected that the picture cannot possibly date from 1444. But nothing prevented Federigo

THE FLAGELLATION. (23¼×31¾″) GALLERIA NAZIONALE
DELLE MARCHE, URBINO.
PAGE 48: THE FLAGELLATION, DETAIL, LEFT SIDE.
PAGE 49: THREE BYSTANDERS, DETAIL, RIGHT SIDE.

—or someone else—from ordering it many years afterwards,
as a memento of an event that had not been forgotten. The new
interpretation proposed by Sir Kenneth is that of an allegory
of the humiliations suffered by the Christian Church upon the
taking of Constantinople by the Turks in 1453, and painted on
the occasion of some eccleciastical council called about that

49

time, perhaps the Council of Mantua in 1459. But the traditional account of the meaning behind the picture rings truer, it seems to me, than such explanations as this, which, though by no means far-fetched, has no historical evidence to support it.

Except for early guide books to Urbino, which mention it as being in the sacristy of the Cathedral, there is no reference to *The Flagellation* in contemporary records.

The work is legibly signed: OPVS PETRI DE BVRGO SANCTI SEPVLCRI. Also mentioned in the guide books just referred to is another inscription: *Convenerunt in unum*. But as it is no longer to be seen, it must have been on the frame, now lost. This same inscription, as a matter of fact, always referring to the episode of the Flagellation, is to be found in many illuminated codices.

II

THE FRESCO CYCLE OF THE STORY OF THE TRUE CROSS

CHURCH OF SAN FRANCESCO, AREZZO

VIEW OF OUR PHOTOGRAPHER AT WORK IN THE CHAPEL.
CHURCH OF SAN FRANCESCO, AREZZO.

To photograph the frescos of Piero della Francesca in the Church of San Francesco at Arezzo, we had to erect a scaffolding nearly fifty feet high, shown here from just beyond the altar at the entrance of the chapel. This was the only way of getting "close-ups" of each and every section of the vast fresco sequence. Thus even outlying details, usually hidden in the shadows of the church, are brought out with the same clean-cut clarity with which the artist saw them on the day he painted them.

Some five hundred years have passed since Piero della Francesca, precariously perched with his assistants on a scaffolding probably even more fragile than this one, peopled the broad expanse of wall with the creations of his mind, creatures made strangely concrete and full-bodied. As his eye travels from scene to scene, the visitor to San Francesco must soon be lost in contemplative admiration of their strict, harmonious sequence and the stalwart grandeur of the figures, taken singly or in groups. We include these photographs in hopes of evoking something of the atmosphere that reigns between these high painted walls. On either side we see the frescos rising in broad tiers, with the serried battle-pieces on the lowest register, a pageant of majestic scenes and majestic figures whose serene timelessness is one of the summits of artistic expression. As he pauses over the color plates in the following pages, the reader will thus be able to visualize them in their architectural setting.

FRESCOS ON THE LEFTHAND WALL OF THE CHAPEL.
CHURCH OF SAN FRANCESCO, AREZZO.

FRESCOS ON THE RIGHTHAND WALL OF THE CHAPEL.
CHURCH OF SAN FRANCESCO, AREZZO.

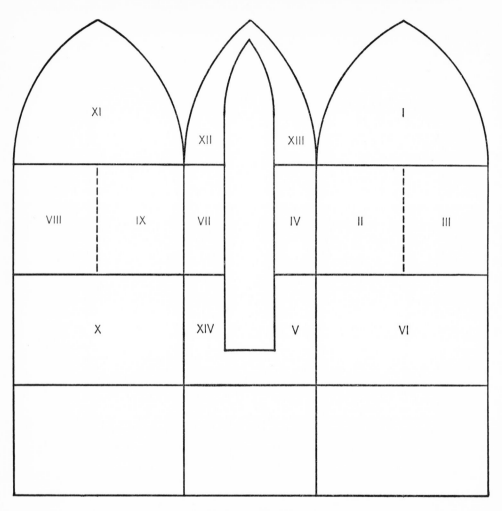

PLAN OF THE FRESCOS
IN THE CHURCH OF SAN FRANCESCO, AREZZO.

SEQUENCE
OF THE DIFFERENT SCENES

I
THE DEATH OF ADAM

II-III
THE QUEEN OF SHEBA WORSHIPPING THE WOOD OF THE CROSS
THE QUEEN OF SHEBA BEING RECEIVED BY KING SOLOMON

IV
THE CARRYING OF THE WOOD OF THE CROSS

V
THE DREAM OF CONSTANTINE

VI
THE VICTORY OF CONSTANTINE OVER MAXENTIUS

VII
THE TORTURE OF JUDAS

VIII-IX
THE FINDING OF THE CROSS
THE REVEALING OF THE TRUE CROSS

X
THE VICTORY OF HERACLIUS OVER CHOSROES

XI
HERACLIUS RESTORING THE CROSS TO JERUSALEM

XII
A PROPHET

XIII
A PROPHET

XIV
THE ANNUNCIATION

THE FRESCOS AT AREZZO

Dating, as explained, from between 1452 and 1466, the cycle of frescos relating *The Story of the True Cross* in the choir of the Church of San Francesco at Arezzo constitutes Piero's major work, and makes this small Tuscan town a privileged place of pilgrimage today for modern-minded artists and art-lovers from all over the world.

Piero must have felt a little cramped by the Gothic architecture of the surfaces allotted him to work on. In order to set the stage, as it were, for the scenes he had in mind, he had to divide up not only the side walls into three broad tiers, but also the back wall on either side of the tall narrow window. Taking these well-defined areas, he then opened them out, like so many windows giving on to a calm and monumental world.

On the two side walls the nature of the scenes themselves is consistently adapted to this division into superimposed tiers. Along the lower level, on either side of the chapel, we find the two "battle-pieces," which, with their serried groups of figures and over-all density, serve as a kind of foundation for the upper scenes to stand on. Along the second level are the more spacious ceremonial scenes: *The Queen of Sheba's Visit to King Solomon* on one side, to the right, and on the opposite wall *The Finding of the Cross*. Here, with the figures strung out at slight intervals, the impression we get is almost one of lightness, as compared with the "battles" below them. On the third and topmost level, painted in the lunettes just below the vaulting, are *The Death of Adam*, on the right, and then *Heraclius Restoring the Cross to Jerusalem*, on the left; figures are sparsely scattered and the broad stretch of open sky dominates, conveying an almost aerial effect. The artist's aim was obviously to move upwards in a kind of architectural progression from base to lunette, as his sense of harmony and proportion dictated.

—   —

THE DEATH OF ADAM (NO. I ON THE PLAN), LOWER PART. THE STORY
OF THE TRUE CROSS. FRESCO, CHURCH OF SAN FRANCESCO, AREZZO.

But radical difficulties lay in wait at the back of the choir, where the tall center window called for a different lay-out altogether. Moreover, the "luminist" technique of *The Dream of Constantine*, on the right, could hardly be expected to hold its own, architecturally speaking, against the massive solidity of *The Annunciation*, to the left on the same level. On the other hand, strict balance was not really essential here, in view of the narrower, more homogeneous strips of wall-space on which the scenes had to be painted.

Perhaps the best-known frescos are those on the right wall, beginning with *The Death of Adam*, in the lunette. The silent group of figures, standing in filial awe around the old man as he lies dying, is one of the loftiest creations in all art, with its rhythmic undercurrent of something yet to come, a pure state of contemplation inseparable from the presence of death. An inner tension is set up in each figure, but quite naturally, without any gesturing or show of emotion.

The double scene of *The Queen of Sheba's Visit to King
Solomon*, immediately below, is exceptionally fine, even for the
Arezzo frescos, so perfect is the balance of spatial depth and
surface elements, so magnificent and satisfying the transcendental
beauty of the Queen of Sheba's retinue.

On the lower register of the back wall to the right we find *The Victory of Constantine*, a model of transposition, an ostensible battle scene having become a vision of knights on parade in which sheer beauty vies with dauntless power, amid an intricate play of solid volumes, heraldic charges, fluttering banners and interwoven pikes and horses' legs.

THE DEATH OF ADAM, DETAIL, LEFT SIDE. THE STORY OF THE TRUE CROSS. FRESCO, CHURCH OF SAN FRANCESCO, AREZZO.

Despite their fine qualities, both *The Victory of Heraclius over Chosroes* and *The Finding of the Cross*, on the lower and middle levels of the lefthand wall, are less free in treatment. But for all their formal abstraction, we find an abundance of striking details in them. In the lunette, *Heraclius Restoring the Cross to Jerusalem* smacks a little too obviously of anecdote.

Another group of masterpieces covers the narrow vertical strips of wall next to the window. One of the finest is the *Prophet* on the upper right, typical of Piero at his best—a magnificent upright figure whose stalwart form amply vouches for his moral integrity, and vice versa. In the first scene on the left, *The Annunciation*, the Virgin stands like a tall, flawless column, impassibly majestic and noble. Here we are far indeed from the stock psychology of paleness and timorous delicacy applied by generations of painters to the Virgin. Piero's women, spiritually and physically, are as robust as his architecture. On the lower right, next the window, is *The Dream of Constantine*, Piero's night-piece. With the cone-shaped tent and the sturdy horizontal formed by the bedstead, he succeeds in infusing architectural strength even into the silvery light, which hangs motionless, without a hint of vibration, an island in the night. This is a picture the eye alone cannot cope with. It is the last word we can expect from the creative imagination and the organizing genius of an artist. Let me add what I today am convinced of: unprecedented before or since, *The Dream of Constantine* is a work that stands alone and apart in the entire history of art. And why is this so? Its uniqueness consists, perhaps, in a deliberate circumscribing, or concentration, of its power to *represent*, with an immense increase in its power of *being*, instinct as it is with life-forces whose poetry and vague terrors the scene somehow reveals. Most extraordinary of all, perhaps, is the light, whose presence is as real as that of a solid body, a miraculous transmutation of the intangible.

THE QUEEN OF SHEBA WORSHIPPING THE WOOD OF THE CROSS
(NO. 2 ON THE PLAN).
THE STORY OF THE TRUE CROSS.
FRESCO, CHURCH OF SAN FRANCESCO, AREZZO.

PAGE 66: THE QUEEN OF SHEBA WORSHIPPING THE WOOD OF THE CROSS.
DETAIL OF HER RETINUE.
THE STORY OF THE TRUE CROSS. CHURCH OF SAN FRANCESCO, AREZZO.

THE QUEEN OF SHEBA BEING RECEIVED BY KING SOLOMON
(NO. 3 ON THE PLAN).
THE STORY OF THE TRUE CROSS.
FRESCO, CHURCH OF SAN FRANCESCO, AREZZO.

PAGE 67: THE QUEEN OF SHEBA BEING RECEIVED BY KING SOLOMON.
DETAIL OF HER RETINUE.
THE STORY OF THE TRUE CROSS. CHURCH OF SAN FRANCESCO, AREZZO.

What has already been said of his use of color in general also holds good for the Arezzo frescos. A few examples, however, will give us a better idea of the relationship he sets up between color and light. *The Queen of Sheba worshipping the Wood of the Cross* is perhaps most revealing because of its excellent state of preservation. To the left, in the retinue behind the kneeling Queen, the harmony of tones is made up of pink (second lady-in-waiting), white and red (first lady) and blue (the Queen). In *The Queen of Sheba being received by King Solomon,* the first figure is wearing red, the second pink and blue-grey, Solomon white and sky-blue, the Queen of Sheba white, her first lady-in-waiting green and the second pink. Now painters who stress light and tonal qualities usually keep to a narrow range of colors. Piero is a striking exception to the rule. He covers the spectrum, taking delight in fine harmonies of tone and calling on color for the wistful accent of spring and renascent tenderness he often seeks for in his art. Sown amid these color harmonies, his light overlays them with its magic.

The frescos were restored in 1860 by Gaetano Bianchi, and again recently by Domenico Fiscali, but their present state is far from satisfactory. Two watercolor replicas by Antoine Ramboux (1790-1866), painted between 1816 and 1842, give some idea of the frescos as they were before serious deterioration had set in, due to damp. Now in the Academy at Düsseldorf, these two watercolors were published by Warburg in the Acts of the Tenth International Congress of the History of Art, Rome 1922, pp. 326-327.

THE QUEEN OF SHEBA BEING RECEIVED BY KING SOLOMON. THE STORY ▶
OF THE TRUE CROSS. FRESCO, CHURCH OF SAN FRANCESCO, AREZZO.

PAGE 69: DETAIL OF THE QUEEN OF SHEBA AND KING SOLOMON.
PAGE 70: DETAIL OF FIGURES IN KING SOLOMON'S RETINUE.
PAGE 71: DETAIL OF FIGURES IN THE QUEEN OF SHEBA'S RETINUE.

THE STORY OF THE TRUE CROSS

It would, of course, be a mistake to lay stress on the importance of the subject in Piero's work. Nevertheless, if the great frescos at Arezzo are to be fully appreciated, some idea must be had of the narrative on which they are based.

The story of the True Cross is a pure creation of the mediaeval mind. It adroitly combines several very old legends, one as recounted in the apocryphal *Gospel of Nicodemus*, and two others from the *Golden Legend* of Jacopo Voragine. As early as 1380, or thereabouts, Agnolo Gaddi painted a cycle of frescos on these legends in the Church of Santa Croce at Florence. *The Story of the True Cross* was, as a matter of fact, a popular theme in all the figurative arts of the Middle Ages and the Renaissance.

In Piero's frescos the tale begins in the large lunette on the righthand wall (no. 1 on the plan). Hoary with age, feeling death at hand, Adam calls upon his son Seth to fetch the Balm of Mercy, promised him long ago by the Angel of the Earthly Paradise (right side). Seth goes and the angel gives him a sprig of the Tree of Life, bidding him plant it in Adam's mouth after the old man's death (left side). Before long a tree had sprung up (center), and by the time King David reigned its wood had already worked many miracles. Though thrown into the Piscina Probatica, the wood continued to prove its immense healing power. Hoping to rid themselves of it for good and be left in peace, the Jews used the wood to build a small bridge over the stream called Siloam.

Then the Queen of Sheba journeyed to Jerusalem to see King Solomon. When she came to the bridge, knowing of its miraculous nature, she knelt down and worshipped the wood.

THE DREAM OF CONSTANTINE (NO. 5 ON THE PLAN). THE STORY OF THE TRUE ▶
CROSS. FRESCO, CHURCH OF SAN FRANCESCO, AREZZO.

THE VICTORY OF CONSTANTINE OVER MAXENTIUS (NO. 6 ON THE PLAN), LEFT SIDE. THE STORY OF THE TRUE CROSS. SAN FRANCESCO, AREZZO.

And when she stood before King Solomon in his Royal Palace, to him and his assembled courtiers she prophesied: "For this sacred wood all the earth will tremble, sun and moon will grow dark, and the veil within the Temple will be rent from top to bottom, and many saints will rise again and be seen in Jerusalem. O Solomon, how ill thou hast cared for this Holy Wood!"

THE VICTORY OF CONSTANTINE OVER MAXENTIUS, LANDSCAPE DETAIL
ON THE RIGHT. THE STORY OF THE TRUE CROSS. SAN FRANCESCO, AREZZO.

The wood was destined to become the Cross of Calvary on which the Son of Man should suffer crucifixion after completing his mission on earth (symbolized perhaps by *The Annunciation*, no. 14). When Christ was judged and condemned, the Jews seized on the wood of the bridge over the Siloam for the making of the Cross, which they carried triumphantly into Jerusalem (no. 4). Once the divine sacrifice was over, the Cross was buried in the earth, where it remained for more than two hundred years.

A day came when, led by the tyrant Maxentius, an armed multitude stood at the gates of Rome. The peril was great, and within the city the Emperor Constantine feared for the worst. Then in the night an angel appeared to him. Starting from his sleep and lifting up his eyes, he saw a cross shining in the sky, on which he read these words: *In signo hoc confide et vinces* (no. 5). Taking comfort from this vision, the Roman Emperor had an emblem made, representing the cross as he had seen it in the night sky. And holding it before him in his outstretched hand, he advanced at the head of his troops. Maxentius rode forth with his men, but near the river the hand of God stopped him short and he fled without giving battle (no. 6).

Constantine now embraced Christianity and sent his mother, St Helena, to Jerusalem in search of the True Cross. Reaching the Holy City, she sought in vain for its hiding-place. No one knew where it lay, save for a Jew by the name of Judas, who refused to give up the secret, for fear of jeopardizing his own faith. St Helena had him put at the bottom of a dry well and left him there to fast for six days. On the seventh day Judas asked to be brought up (no. 7). This being done, he led St Helena to the Mount of Calvary, where the Cross had been buried, together with those on which the two thieves had died.

◄ THE VICTORY OF CONSTANTINE OVER MAXENTIUS, DETAIL OF CONSTANTINE'S HEAD. THE STORY OF THE TRUE CROSS. CHURCH OF SAN FRANCESCO, AREZZO.

THE FINDING OF THE CROSS (NO. 8 ON THE PLAN). THE STORY OF THE TRUE
CROSS. FRESCO, CHURCH OF SAN FRANCESCO, AREZZO.

THE REVEALING OF THE TRUE CROSS (NO. 9 ON THE PLAN), DETAIL, ▶
RIGHT SIDE. THE STORY OF THE TRUE CROSS. SAN FRANCESCO, AREZZO.

A temple had been built on the spot, but when this was razed and the ground cleared, Judas himself set to digging and the three crosses were soon unearthed (no. 8). But how was the True Cross to be distinguished from the others?

THE FINDING OF THE CROSS. DETAIL: THE CITY OF JERUSALEM. THE STORY OF THE TRUE CROSS. FRESCO, CHURCH OF SAN FRANCESCO, AREZZO.

That very day a youth had died at Jerusalem. One by one the three crosses were lowered over his body. As the third one came down, the True Cross, he rose to life again (no. 9). Before such a miracle as this, no doubts could remain. Even Judas underwent a change of heart; he was baptized a Christian and in time became the Bishop of Jerusalem under the name of Quiriacus.

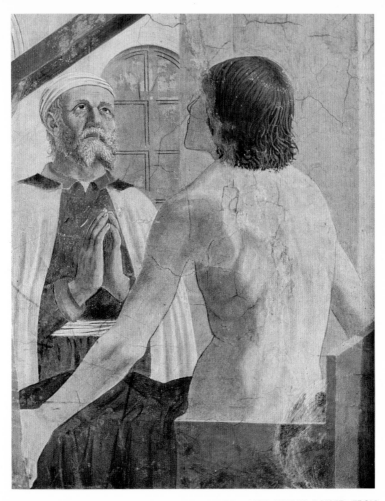

THE REVEALING OF THE TRUE CROSS. DETAIL: THE YOUTH RAISED FROM
THE DEAD. THE STORY OF THE TRUE CROSS. SAN FRANCESCO, AREZZO.

In 615, as a punitive measure, Christ allowed Chosroes, King of the Persians, to subdue all the kingdoms of the earth. After having taken Jerusalem, Chosroes carried off the Holy Cross to his own palace, where he made it the ornament of his throne room (no. 10, right side). Appalled at this sacrilege, the Roman Emperor Heraclius gathered an army together and met him in battle on the banks of the Danube (no. 10, left and center). Soundly beaten, Chosroes was beheaded in front of his throne (no. 10, right side). Barefoot, in the garb of the humblest pilgrim, Heraclius brought the True Cross back to Jerusalem. It re-entered the Holy City, miraculously enough, by the very gate through which Christ had borne it out on His shoulders, on the day of the Passion (no. 11).

THE AREZZO FRESCOS
IN THE LIGHT OF ART-CRITICISM

In view of the exceptional magnitude and quality of these frescos, Arezzo is usually regarded as Piero della Francesca's chief center of activity. Like nearby Borgo San Sepolcro, his native town, Arezzo is located in the southernmost part of Tuscany. Thus it is wrong to assimilate Piero to the Umbrian painters. His art, furthermore, has nothing in common with that of Perugino, the very prototype of Umbrian artists. The truth is that he falls naturally into line with the great Tuscan tradition.

During his lifetime, as we have seen, he enjoyed none of the fame and favors lavished on the Florentine masters, for Arezzo was an outlying provincial town. Though it flourished in the Middle Ages, it had soon lagged behind the great cultural centers of the Renaissance. Its attraction today is precisely the

THE VICTORY OF HERACLIUS OVER CHOSROES (NO. 10 ON THE PLAN), ▶
DETAIL. THE STORY OF THE TRUE CROSS. CHURCH OF SAN FRANCESCO, AREZZO.

fresco cycle relating *The Story of the True Cross* in San Francesco, and little else. Thanks to them, this church has come to vie with the Vatican Stanze and the Sistine Chapel. But things were very different in former times; then only occasional visitors wandered into the smaller towns off the beaten paths that led to Rome and Florence, where Piero's works were almost lost to view amidst an abundance of art treasures.

THE VICTORY OF HERACLIUS OVER CHOSROES, DETAILS. THE STORY OF THE TRUE CROSS. FRESCO, CHURCH OF SAN FRANCESCO, AREZZO.

Most of his contemporary admirers were men who appreciated his geometry. It is true that Giorgio Vasari, born nineteen years after his death, and himself the son of one of Piero's pupils, lauds him with unqualified admiration. But thereafter a shroud of silent neglect fell over his art and his name. This was natural enough in the 17th and 18th centuries, when even those who were acquainted with his work were quite incapable of understanding it, for it met none of the criteria that shaped taste in

THE VICTORY OF HERACLIUS OVER CHOSROES, DETAILS.
THE STORY OF THE TRUE CROSS. FRESCO.
CHURCH OF SAN FRANCESCO, AREZZO.

those days, neither aspiring to an ideal beauty after the manner of Raphael, nor conforming to classically established rules of composition. But its gravest, most unforgivable shortcoming, in the eyes of men two hundred years ago, must have been its complete absence of elaborate baroque convolutions. Even

HERACLIUS RESTORING THE CROSS TO JERUSALEM (NO. 11 ON THE PLAN), DETAILS. THE STORY OF THE TRUE CROSS. SAN FRANCESCO, AREZZO.

the revival of interest in "primitives" early in the 19th century failed to rescue him from oblivion. The German philologist and aesthetician Von Rumohr, in his *Italienische Forschungen* (1827–1832) dismissed his work as destitute of interest. At that time the term "primitive" was applied chiefly to Perugino, and Piero's art, utterly devoid of sentimentality, continued to pass unnoticed. Later exponents of realism found the vigor of his form to their liking, but were put off by his geometry.

It was Bernhard Berenson, in 1897, who saw that the greatness of Piero's forms and figures lay in their impersonality, their emotionlessness. But he felt that the rigor of his perspective left a flaw in his achievements, and that, for this reason, his works fell short of true beauty. In a recent essay, Mr Berenson has revised his judgment, waiving his former reservations. Developing the idea of impersonality in Piero's art, he deduces from it a definition of universal art as being one that *is* and *exists*, and does not merely *represent* and *express*. Since the beginning of this century, many monographs have been devoted to Piero, the most exhaustive being that of Roberto Longhi.

The fact remains that all the critics' spadework has so far failed to give rise to any popular enthusiasm for Piero's art. The public has been only partially won over. Nevertheless, his art follows the same clearly marked line towards abstraction along which the best artists of the past sixty years have consistently developed, particularly the Cubists, whose works frequently hark back to the great frescoes at Arezzo. All those who take the hint and go there will discover for themselves the unique figure Piero della Francesca cuts in art. The fascination he has for us today can only increase as time goes on. Other syntheses are possible, obviously, between the factual and the visionary, and those of other artists may seem to some more plausible than Piero's. But none can challenge the sovereign authority with which he joins the real and the ideal into one.

HERACLIUS RESTORING THE CROSS TO JERUSALEM (NO. 11 ON THE PLAN),
DETAIL. THE STORY OF THE TRUE CROSS.
FRESCO, CHURCH OF SAN FRANCESCO, AREZZO.

THE ANNUNCIATION (NO. 14 ON THE PLAN). THE STORY OF THE TRUE CROSS.
FRESCO, CHURCH OF SAN FRANCESCO, AREZZO.

92

III

THE RESURRECTION

Palazzo Comunale, Borgo San Sepolcro

THIS is another of those masterpieces hardly surpassed even by Piero himself, despite the fact that, for an artist by no means enamored of movement, the Resurrection seems like a strange subject to choose. In dealing with it, even Giotto had made a praiseworthy effort to render figures in movement. But Piero would have none of this, and went ahead with no discernible qualms, painting figures more steadfastly calm than ever.

In the foreground are soldiers seen in foreshortening, which is normally a typical device for suggesting movement. But not for Piero, who so crystallizes these figures that their forms literally become a hundred light-reflecting facets. We might almost read an image into their many-sidedness: the arabesque made by the spokes of a wheel, but a wheel that is rooted in eternity and will never move again. Nor will Christ, fixed for all time in his inviolable sacredness; only his upraised leg reminds us that he is issuing from the tomb, and supposed to be moving. The compact group forms a pyramid, surmounted by the head of Christ, with the slumbering centurions as its broad base. We may note that all the figures are laid out strictly in terms of their light relationships. The soldiers are dark and Christ is luminous, a contrast echoed in the dark landscape standing out against a bright sky. The symbolism is obvious: Christ and the heavens glow with light, while men fend for themselves in earthly darkness. And if so potent a spell emanates from the scene, this is because Piero has succeeded in making a symbolic apparition hauntingly real, bringing an abstract vision down to earth.

THE RESURRECTION. FRESCO, PALAZZO COMUNALE,
BORGO SAN SEPOLCRO.

The relationship between figures and landscape is every-where calculated to enhance the spiritual potency of the composition, and to assert man's supremacy over nature.

Mentioned by Vasari as the artist's finest work at Borgo San Sepolcro, there is reason to believe that it was removed from its original emplacement in 1480. It may have been covered over with a coat of whitewash in the 18th century. The first reference to it in modern times comes from Rosini (1839), who ascribed it to Signorelli. Critics today regard it as belonging to Piero's final phase, contemporary, that is, with the Arezzo frescos.

THE RESURRECTION, DETAIL. PALAZZO COMUNALE, BORGO SAN SEPOLCRO.

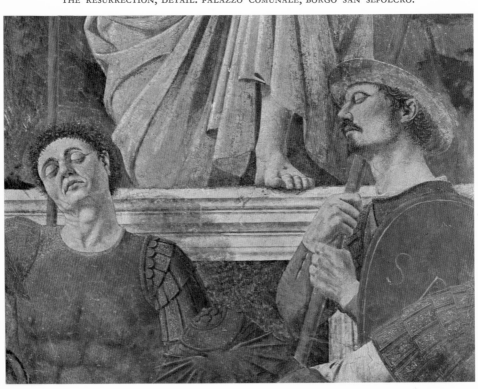

DIPTYCH OF FEDERIGO DA MONTEFELTRO
AND BATTISTA SFORZA

Uffizi, Florence

As we have seen, this diptych must be assumed to date from after 1472, the year of Battista Sforza's death. Adolfo Venturi (*Piero della Francesca*, page 56) described her face as more like a "waxen death-mask" than a portrait. Federigo's portrait, on the other hand, is that of a vigorous man in the prime of life, and his swarthy skin stands out strongly against the blue sky. His profile, like that of Malatesta, winds across the picture-space uninterruptedly, cut out with the sharpness of a chiseled medallion. The landscape behind him is very far away, a vision in the distance, never reaching into the foreground. An interesting point is that the countryside here is totally unlike anything in the region of Urbino; this is an ideal landscape meant to magnify the isolated presence of the profile.

On the back of the portraits are two "triumphs," allegories full of grace and gem-like colors. The procession passes on a rocky terrace, high above a far-flung landscape that poetically re-echoes the main scene. Endlessly winding rivers and conical hills, rhythmically repeated, provocative of nostalgia, create a landscape of ideal peace, ideally proportioned.

Drawn by two white horses, Federigo is escorted by the four Cardinal Virtues: Justice, Prudence, Fortitude and Temperance. Battista Sforza's "float" is drawn by stately unicorns; she is attended by the Theological Virtues: Faith, Hope and Charity.

PAGE 98: BATTISTA SFORZA. LEFT VOLET OF THE DIPTYCH. (EACH PANEL 18½ × 13″) UFFIZI, FLORENCE.

PAGE 99: FEDERIGO DA MONTEFELTRO. RIGHT VOLET OF THE DIPTYCH. (EACH PANEL 18½ × 13″) UFFIZI, FLORENCE.

ALLEGORICAL SCENE. BACK OF THE RIGHT VOLET. UFFIZI, FLORENCE.

Singing his praises (in the present tense), the following Latin verses are inscribed on the back of the right volet, beneath the triumphal car on which Federigo sits:

Clarus insigni vehitur triumpho
Quem parem summis ducibus perhennis
Fama virtutum celebrat decenter
Sceptra tenentem

Peer of the greatest leaders, he is borne in regal triumph, holding the scepter nobly and glorified by the undying fame of his virtues.

ALLEGORICAL SCENE. BACK OF THE LEFT VOLET. UFFIZI, FLORENCE.

This inscription (in the past tense) is found on the back of the volet. Battista Sforza died in 1472. The diptych may have been painted on the occasion of her death, or shortly afterwards.

Quemodum rebus tenuit secundis
Coniugis magni decorata rerum
Laude gestarum volitat per ora
Cuncta virorum

Even as it was with her in her great days, so she still lives on the lips of all men, covered with the glory of her illustrious husband's deeds.

VIRGIN AND CHILD WITH TWO ANGELS

Galleria Nazionale delle Marche, Urbino

THIS picture comes from the Church of Santa Maria delle Grazie near Sinigallia. No surviving records make mention of it, but its superb qualities leave no doubt as to its authenticity, the style being manifestly that of Piero's last phase.

It has been customary to regard Piero's last works as marking a slight decline in his art. Sir Kenneth Clark shares this view and surmises that, towards the end of his life, the artist concentrated on his theories of perspective and geometry to the detriment of his painting. There is no denying that in the last works we see him moving away from the great, ideal forms he had clung to in the past, and from their stately, geometric beauty. But a new development took their place.

From his earliest works onward, he showed himself to be on thoroughly familiar terms with Flemish technique, particularly that of Jan van Eyck. But only in his last works did he strive for—and achieve—a deeper expression of those spiritual states immanent in the play of light and shadow. He came to lay greater stress on shadow, extending its dominion in the picture, and adjusting forms to suit an intensified chiaroscuro. Now, too, he took greater pains over details. It is enough to compare the two angels at Urbino with those in the London *Baptism*. The latter, in their infinite grace, have none of the intense life, none of the moral force that stream from the angels here. The still life and the window behind further emphasize the intricate harmony of the Urbino picture.

This much is certain: far from having entered on a decline, the man who painted such a masterpiece as this must have felt a fresh spurt of creative energy. The most we can read into it otherwise is a soul-struggle of some kind to which Piero may have fallen a prey in the transition from the happy certainties of youth to the misgivings of age. But his capacities as an artist were not at stake.

THE VIRGIN AND CHILD WITH TWO ANGELS. (24×21″)
GALLERIA NAZIONALE DELLE MARCHE, URBINO.

THE NATIVITY
National Gallery, London

I N *The Nativity* we have a further advance in the new style
Piero had embarked on with the Urbino *Virgin and Child*.
Sir Kenneth Clark was the first to point out that the Christchild lying on the ground was directly inspired by the Child
in the *Portinari Triptych* of Hugo van der Goes, now in the
Uffizi. But this is not all that Piero took from Flemish painting
in general, and from the *Portinari Triptych* in particular. Where
else do they come from, the inward, intimate charm of individual
features, of the composition itself, as well as the peculiar type
of landscape and the realistic handling of old men? But Piero
was too strong a personality not to transform them all into
something quite different. And the Virgin, no longer the symbol
of motherhood we found in the Arezzo *Annunciation*, has become
a handsome young woman of humble station kneeling in prayer.
The angels round her, singing the glory of God, are Piero's
deepest, most joyful creations, expressive though they are of
a tender solicitude that verges on mourning. The treatment of
the shelter here is not what previous works would lead us to
expect from Piero. It may well be historically accurate, but this
is precisely what is so surprising.

The monumental breadth of this art certainly suggests pride
in its maker—a monumental pride, that of kings and creator-
gods. Yet not a trace of it shows through in *The Nativity*.
Deflected perhaps from the confident, humanist self-reliance of
early days, did Piero come to need the consolations of faith?
Or having rounded out his mathematical theories to his satisfaction, did he no longer feel impelled to put them to the test
in painting? However this may be, *The Nativity* shows us Piero
unmistakably turning in upon himself, and deliberately forsaking

the great externals of his art, so carefully built up in the past, in order now to explore the furthest reaches of the human soul.

The underdrawing of several figures now shows through. However, the picture is not unfinished, as some have thought, but ravaged by generations of restorers. In spite of everything, its charm and fascination have come through unimpaired.

THE NATIVITY. DETAIL: ANGEL MUSICIANS. NATIONAL GALLERY, LONDON.

In his notes to Vasari, Milanesi mentioned *The Nativity* as belonging to the Marini-Franceschi family of Borgo San Sepolcro, Piero's descendants. In the keeping of Cavaliere Frescobaldi at Florence from about 1848, it was bought by Alexander Barker of London in 1861, then by the National Gallery in 1874.

◀ THE NATIVITY. DETAIL OF THE LANDSCAPE. NATIONAL GALLERY, LONDON.

THE VIRGIN AND CHILD WITH SAINTS AND ANGELS

Pinacoteca di Brera, Milan

T HIS altarpiece came from the Church of San Bernardino at Urbino. Since this church was built after the death of Federigo da Montefeltro—between 1483 and 1491, to be precise—and since, in his will, Federigo expressed his desire to be interred in the Church of San Donato at Urbino, we are faced with the following alternative: either the picture was painted for San Donato and later transferred to San Bernardino, or else Piero painted it after Federigo's death, sometime, that is, between 1483 and 1491. The latter hypothesis is to be preferred, for the simple reason that St Bernardin figures among the six saints, whereas St Donatus does not. (In this connection see the article by P. Rotondi in *Belle Arti*, 1, 3-4, 1947, page 192).

Doubts have been cast on this picture's authenticity, but there is no justification for them. Its qualities are much too fine for it to be by anyone else. Only Federigo's hands—very realistic, but out of keeping with the rest—may be ascribed to a follower of the Flemish painters. Some say Pedro Berruguete, known to have been at Urbino after 1473, where he collaborated with Justus of Ghent in decorating the Duke's Study in the Castle of Urbino, before going back to Spain in 1483.

But even apart from this regrettable intervention the forthright realism of the various figures is unusual for Piero. Its effect is the more acutely felt as the composition as a whole has taken a distinctly abstract turn. The scene is imagined in a marble apse, and all figures stand stiffly erect, the Virgin hieratic almost

THE VIRGIN AND CHILD WITH SAINTS AND ANGELS, AND FEDERIGO ►
DA MONTEFELTRO, DONOR. (97¼×66¾″) PINACOTECA DI BRERA, MILAN.

to the point of distortion. The fact is that, between the realism of faces and certain details of clothing, on the one hand, and the geometrical abstraction of the background and general composition on the other, there is a contrast that becomes an outright clash—one that by no means leaves us convinced or satisfied. But the angels' heads and the wonderfully fine head of St Peter Martyr—believed to be a portrait of Piero's friend, the mathematician Luca Pacioli—more than make up for this when we appraise the work as a whole.

The egg suspended from the ceiling of the apse may be taken purely for the satisfaction given the eye by the perfection of its form, or as a symbol of the four elements of the world (see *Journal of the Warburg and Courtauld Institutes*, vol. IX, page 27) or of the creation.

SELECTED BIBLIOGRAPHY

INDEX OF NAMES
AND BIOGRAPHICAL NOTICES

TABLE OF CONTENTS

SELECTED BIBLIOGRAPHY

The best edition of Piero della Francesca's *De Prospectiva Pingendi* is that of G. Nicco FASOLA, Florence 1942. — G. MANCINI published the artist's *De Corporibus Regularibus* in *Memorie dell'Academia dei Lincei*, Rome 1915.

Giorgio VASARI, *Delle Vite de' piu eccellenti pittori, scultori, ed architettori*, Florence 1550 & 1568; the standard edition is that of MILANESI, Florence 1878-1885. — Roberto LONGHI, *Piero dei Franceschi e lo sviluppo dell'arte veneziana*, in *L'Arte*, XVII, 1914, p. 198-221. — Adolfo VENTURI, *Piero della Francesca*, Florence 1922. — Roberto LONGHI, *Piero della Francesca*, Rome 1927. — Julius SCHLOSSER, in *Xenia*, 1938. — Creighton GILBERT, *New Evidence for the Date of Piero della Francesca's "Count and Countess of Urbino,"* in *Marsyas*, I, 1941, pp. 41-53. — Millard MEISS, *A Documented Altarpiece by Piero della Francesca*, in *The Art Bulletin*, XXIII, I, March 1941, pp. 53-65. — Mario SALMI, *Piero della Francesca e Giuliano Amedei*, in *Rivista d'Arte*, XXIV, January-June 1942, pp. 26-44; *La Bibbia di Borso d'Este e Piero della Francesca*, in *La Rinascita*, July-September 1943, p. 365; *Piero della Francesca e il palazzo ducale di Urbino*, Florence 1945; *Un'ipotesi su Piero della Francesca*, in *Arti Figurative*, April 1947, p. 48. — Kenneth CLARK, *Piero della Francesca's St. Augustine Altarpiece*, in *The Burlington Magazine*, August 1947, p. 205. — J. ALAZARD, *Piero della Francesca*, Paris 1948. — Roberto LONGHI, *Piero in Arezzo*, in *Paragone*, 11, 1950. — Bernhard BERENSON, *Piero della Francesca o dell'arte non eloquente*, Florence 1950. — Kenneth CLARK, *Piero della Francesca*, London 1951. — Roberto LONGHI, *La leggenda della Croce*, Milan 1951. — Henri FOCILLON, *Piero della Francesca*, Paris 1952. — Lionello VENTURI, *Piero della Francesca, G. Seurat, J. Gris*, in *Diogène*, 3, 1953, pp. 25-30.

INDEX AND BIOGRAPHICAL NOTICES

The following historical and biographical notices, relating to predecessors and contemporaries of Piero della Francesca mentioned in the text, were compiled by R. Skira-Venturi.

ADAM 20, 57-62, 72.

AGNELLO Tommaso di Guido dell' 46.

ALBERTI Leon Battista (Genoa 1404?
- Rome 1472) 11, 12, 13, 43;
Treatise on Painting 13.
Celebrated humanist and architect, descendant of a Florentine family living in exile. After studying literature and philosophy, and traveling in France and Germany with Cardinal Albergati, he went to Rome in 1431, to the Papal Court of Eugene IV, and initiated himself into the builder's art. At Florence in 1434, he was soon on familiar terms with the intellectual and artistic élite there and dedicated his treatise *De Pictura* to Brunelleschi. A favorite with the new pope, Nicolas V, he took an active part in the public works that were then changing the face of Rome. Published his best-known work, *De Re Aedificatoria*, in 1450. Called in to work at the Church of San Francesco at Rimini for Sigismondo Malatesta, he swept aside both the original architecture and the work of his predecessors, begun in 1447 in Gothic style, and produced a temple in the purest Renaissance Classical style (Tempio Malatestiano). At Mantua he built the Church of San Sebastiano, at Florence the Palazzo and Loggia Rucellai. He modernized the Church of Santa Maria Novella at Florence and, for the Gonzagas, designed the Church of Sant'Andrea at Mantua. A practicing architect in great demand, he still found time for extensive literary and philosophical writings. Alberti is the leading speaker in the discussions on art, morals and philosophy recorded by Cristoforo Landino.

AMADI Girolamo 29, 40, 41, 43.

AMEDEI Giuliano 35.

ANDREW St 35.

ANGELICO Fra (Vicchio di Mugello, Tuscany 1387 - Rome 1455) 20. His real name was Giovanni da Fiesole. At 20 he entered the Dominican Monastery of Fiesole, where he seems to have been trained as a painter and illuminator. Much influenced by Lorenzo Monaco. In 1433 the Arte dei Linaioli commissioned a large altarpiece from him, still regarded as one of his finest works. Vasari had it that he painted angels " so beautiful that they seem indeed creatures of paradise." When in 1436 Lorenzo de' Medici made over the church and cloister of San Marco at Florence to the Dominican monks of Fiesole, the restoration of the buildings was entrusted to Michelozzo and the decorations to Fra Angelico. Seconded by his assistants, he painted the walls with scenes from the life of Christ. When the Monastery was inaugurated in 1442 in the presence of Eugene IV, Fra Angelico's work made a vivid impression on the pope, who invited him to Rome. There he painted frescos, now lost, in the Chapel of the Holy Sacrament at the Vatican. After working for several years at Orvieto, he returned to the Vatican to paint frescos in the Chapel of Nicolas V.

Arezzo 18, 23, 25-27, 82, 90; Church of San Francesco 5, 8, 10, 14, 18, 20, 25, 51-92, 96, 104.
ARISTOTLE 11.

BACCI family 25.
Baltimore, Museum of 16.
BARKER Alexander 107.
BENEDETTO Marco di (Piero's brother) 24, 35.
BERENSON Bernhard 90.
Berlin, Museum of 16.
BERNARDIN St 35, 108.

BERRUGUETE Pedro (Paredes de Nava, Castile ca. 1450 - Avila 1504) 108. It is thought that he came to know of Flemish techniques through Fernando Gallego, as he had fully assimilated these by the time he appeared in Italy (before 1477), where he worked with Melozzo da Forli for Federigo da Montefeltro. He joined with Justus of Ghent to paint the figures of prophets and philosophers in the Duke's Study at Urbino. The portrait of Federigo with his son Guidobaldo is also ascribed to him. With the Duke dead in 1482, records show him to be back in Spain in 1483, where he painted many altarpieces in the churches of Castile, the Dominican monasteries and Avila Cathedral. He was the father of the great sculptor Alonso Berruguete.
BIANCHI Gaetano 68.
BICCI DI LORENZO (Florence 1373 - 1452) 25.
A minor painter whose large output shows the influence first of Agnolo Gaddi, then of Lorenzo Monaco and Gentile da Fabriano, whose Quaratesi altarpiece inspired Bicci's *Virgin* in the Galleria Nazionale, Parma. He worked extensively at Florence, Empoli, Pescia, and at the Church of San

Francesco, Arezzo, where he painted the vaulting and the main arch of the choir which, after his death, was decorated by Piero della Francesca.
Borgo San Sepolcro 17, 18, 23, 24, 26, 27, 30-36, 82, 96, 107; Abbey Church, Chapel of the Madonna 27; Badia 27; Cathedral 36; Church of San Rocco 35; Palazzo Comunale 24, 30-35, 94-96; Priory of San Giovanni Battista 36; Sant' Agostino 23, 25, 27; Town Council 23, 26.

BRAMANTE (Monte Asdrualdo, near Urbino 1444 - Rome 1514) 26. Considered the greatest architect of the early 16th century and exponent of the Renaissance Classical style. In the service of Ludovico il Moro at Milan, he rebuilt the Church of San Satiro, contributed to the building of Pavia Cathedral, and oversaw the decorations for Ludovico's sumptuous festivals. After painting some frescos in the Casa Panigarola, Milan (now the Pinacoteca di Brera) and building the central part of the Church of Santa Maria delle Grazie (1492-1497), he left for Rome in 1499. In 1503 he built the round temple (the Tempietto) in the cloister of San Pietro in Montorio, one of the jewels of Renaissance architecture. That same year Julius II became pope and put him in charge of work in progress on St Peter's, the Vatican palace and other buildings in Rome and Loreto. Razing the old basilica, Bramante began work on the new St Peter's in 1506, designing the church in the form of a Greek cross with a semicircular choir, transepts and, in the center, a massive dome upheld by four colossal piers. At his death in 1514 only the four piers and the semicircular arches had been finished. Work thereafter came to a virtual stop; the building plans were tinkered with and continually revised until Michelangelo took charge in 1546.Reverting to Bramante's original design, he declared: "Breaking with Bramante means breaking with truth."

BRUNELLESCHI Filippo (Florence 1379 - 1446) 13.

Articled to a goldsmith as a boy, he developed into a skilled craftsman and sculptor. With two panels representing the *Sacrifice of Abraham*, he competed for a commission to sculpture the bronze doors of the Florentine Baptistery (won by Ghiberti). Thereafter he devoted himself to architecture. Consulted about roofing the choir of Santa Maria del Fiore, he submitted designs for an awe-inspiring dome that had no need of wooden armatures to hold it up. Both his and Ghiberti's designs were accepted and, after considerable wrangling, building of the dome began in 1420 and was finished in 1436, except for the lantern on the top, added after his death. All his contemporaries paid homage to the beauty and daring of the work, one of the great feats of Renaissance architecture. Among other buildings at Florence designed by Brunelleschi are the Spedale degli Innocenti (1421-1424); the Sacristy and Church of San Lorenzo, commissioned by Cosimo de' Medici; the Church of Santa Maria degli Angioli, unfinished for lack of funds; the Church of Santo Spirito; the Palazzo and Villa Pitti at Rusciano, later altered. The first to supplant Gothic, Brunelleschi was the creator of the Renaissance Classical style. Painters are indebted to him for working out the rules of perspective.

BRUNI Leonardo (Arezzo 1370 - Florence 1444) 11, 12.

Became a citizen of Florence in 1416, where he took an active part in political life: ambassador of the Florentine Republic to the Papal Court of Martin V and Chancelor of the Signoria from 1427 until his death. One of the leading humanists in the time of Cosimo de' Medici, connoisseur and popularizer of classical culture, writer, historian and orator, Bruni also championed the use of the vernacular tongue. Nevertheless his Latin translations of the Greek classics were widely read in Renaissance times, as were his historical works, notably the *Historiae Florentini Populi*. Bernardo Rossellino designed his tomb in the Church of Santa Croce.

CASTIGLIONE Sabba da (Milan 1480 - Faenza 1554) 26.

A descendant of the family of which Baldassare Castiglione is the best-known member. Joining the Knights of St John of Jerusalem (Knights of Malta), he fought against the Turks in Rhodes from 1505 to 1508. Returning to Rome, he was named Bursar of the Order. Receiving the commendam of Santa Maria Maddalena at Faenza for his services, he retired to that town in 1517. There he lived until his death, devoting himself to charitable works and collecting rare books and *objets d'art*. His *Ricordi ovvero Ammaestramenti* may still be read; it treats of the moral life and accomplishments of a gentleman, and contains some shrewd observations on the art of his time. Cesena 46; Library 24.

CHOSROES, King of the Persians 21, 57, 63, 82-87.

CLARK Sir Kenneth 46, 47, 102, 104.

Compagnia dell'Annunziata (Arezzo) 25, 27.

Compagnia della Misericordia (Borgo San Sepolcro) 24, 27, 35.

Confraternità di San Bartolomeo (Borgo San Sepolcro) 27.

CONSTANTINE, emperor 10, 21, 57, 59, 62, 63, 72-77.

Constantinople 47.

COROT Camille 21.

Council of Florence 10.
Oecumenical council first convened at Basel in 1431, adjourned in 1437, convoked again at Ferrara in 1438, transferred in 1439 to Florence —hence its name—and adjourned for good in Rome in 1443. The Byzantine Emperor John VII Palaeologus and Patriarch Joseph of Constantinople took part. Among other decisions taken was that of uniting the Greek and Latin Churches.

Council of Mantua 50.

Danube 82.

DAVID, King 72.

DOMENICO VENEZIANO (Venice? - Florence 1461) 18-20, 23, 24.
The date of his birth is unknown and information about his life and activity is very meager. He signed "Domenicus de Veneciis," which proves that he was Venetian. At Florence in 1439, where he stayed until 1445, painting fresco decorations in Sant'Egidio (Santa Maria Nuova) with the help of several assistants, one of them Piero della Francesca. These frescos no longer exist. His only surviving works are the signed *Altarpiece of Santa Lucia* (center panel in the Uffizi) and several fresco fragments, one of them signed, in the National Gallery, London. With these to go on, several other paintings are also ascribed to him.

DONATUS St 108.

Düsseldorf, Academy 68.

ESTE Borso d' (Ferrara 1413-1471) 24.
Natural son of Duke Nicola III and Stella dell'Assassino, his favorite mistress, Borso became the undisputed ruler of Ferrara after the death of his brother Lionello. For 21 years he governed the Duchies of Modena, Reggio and Ferrara. Versed in all the arts of war and a great hunter, he was justly celebrated as a generous, loyal, pleasure-loving lord. Though not particularly cultivated, he patronized the arts, and the Carthusian Monastery of Ferrara and the second storey of the Palazzo Schifanoia (with its frescos in his honor by Tura and Cossa) are due to his munificence. He took delight in miniatures and the *Bible of Borso d'Este* (Biblioteca Estense, Modena) stands as one of the handsomest illuminated books of the Renaissance.

EYCK Jan Van (see VAN EYCK).

FASOLA Nicco, his edition of Piero della Francesca's *De Prospectiva Pingendi* 16.

FERABÒ, 15th-century humanist from Verona 26.

Ferrara 23, 24; Palace 24.

FISCALI Domenico 68.

Flemish painting 19, 102, 104, 108.

Florence 12, 18, 19, 23, 24, 82, 85, 107; Brancacci Chapel 15, 19; Church of Santa Croce 72; Church of Sant'Egidio 24; Uffizi 14, 26, 97-101, 104.

FOCILLON Henri 20.

FRANCESCHI Benedetto de' (Piero's father) 24.

FRESCOBALDI, Cavaliere 107.

GADDI Agnolo (Florence? - 1396) 72.
Son of Taddeo Gaddi, who was a
pupil and assistant of Giotto, Agnolo
decorated the choir of the Church of
Santa Croce at Florence with frescos
on *The Story of the True Cross*, painted
sometime after 1374. Another cycle of
frescos by him, *The Life of the Virgin*,
is in the Chapel of the Holy Girdle in
Prato Cathedral.

GARIN E., *Umanesimo italiano* 11.

GENTILE DA FABRIANO (Fabriano,
  Marches ca. 1370 - Rome 1427) 41.
First referred to in 1408, as painting
an altarpiece for one Francesco Amadi
at Venice, where he also decorated the
Ducal Palace and left his mark on the
whole of Venetian painting. At Bres-
cia from 1414 to 1419, working for
Pandolfo Malatesta. Enrolled in the
Painters' Guild at Florence in 1422.
Finished *The Adoration of the Magi*
(Uffizi, Florence) in 1423 and the
Quaratesi Altarpiece (Uffizi and Natio-
nal Gallery, London) in 1425. Worked
at Siena and Orvieto, then in Rome
in 1427, where he painted frescos on
The Life of St John the Baptist, now
lost, in St John Lateran. He and
Pisanello are the best exponents of
International Gothic in Italy.

GIOTTO (Colle Vespignano, near
  Florence ca. 1267 - Florence 1336)
  94.
Legend and anecdote have almost
overshadowed the little we know of
Giotto's life. The facts are essentially
as follows. In 1312 he was a member
of the Painters' Guild at Florence.
His first known work—painted, as far
as can be determined, in the last years
of the 13th century—is the fresco
cycle on *The Life of St Francis* in the
Upper Church of San Francesco,

Assisi: 28 scenes in the nave, most of
them by Giotto himself, a few by his
pupils. He then made frescos in the
Scrovegni Chapel, Padua, finished in
1305: 37 scenes in three tiers on the
side walls, with *The Last Judgment*
above the entrance and, along the
monochrome plinth, figures of the
Vices and Virtues simulating sculpture. In 1311 he was in Rome in the
service of Cardinal Stefaneschi, for
whom (presumably) he executed a
mosaic, now badly disfigured, and an
altarpiece (Vatican Pinacoteca) whose
style has long been an object of contro-
versy among art-historians. Back in
Florence the same year, he painted a
Crucifix for the Church of Santa
Maria Novella and two pictures of
The Virgin and *The Death of Mary*.
He decorated four chapels in the
Church of Santa Croce; the frescos
in only two of them have survived,
and in very poor condition. In one
chapel he painted *The Lives of St John
the Baptist and St John the Evangelist*,
in the other *The Life of St Francis*.
In 1334 Giotto worked for Robert of
Anjou, King of Naples, the scholar-
friend of Petrarch. Back in Florence
the same year, he was put in charge
of work on the Cathedral. At the same
time building began on the Campanile, designed by him, but he died
before it was finished. He also designed some of the relief-work on the
Campanile. Giotto utterly revolu-
tionized Italian painting.

Vasari, his real name was Tommaso Cassaio, and " Masaccio " a nickname meaning (more or less) " unruly Thomas." He enrolled in the Painters' Guild at Florence in 1422, and in 1426 painted his great altarpiece for the Church of the Carmine, Pisa, now dispersed, the main panels being in the National Gallery, London *(Virgin and Child)*, and the Naples Pinacoteca *(Crucifixion)*. He and Masolino were probably employed by the Carmelite Monastery at Florence when, about 1423, the silk merchant Michele Brancacci commissioned them to decorate the chapel dedicated to the "Madonna of the People" in the Church of Santa Maria del Carmine, Florence. They worked together there until 1427, when Masolino left for Hungary; Masaccio then carried on alone. The following scenes are ascribed to him: *St Peter baptizing*, *St Peter and St John distributing Alms*, *St Peter healing the Sick with his Shadow*, *Adam and Eve cast out of Paradise*, *The Tribute Money* and *St Peter invoking the Holy Spirit*. The last-named fresco was partly repainted by Filippino Lippi, who, some 50 years after Masaccio's death, was called in to complete the decorations.

MATTEO DI GIOVANNI (Borgo San Sepolcro ca. 1430 - Siena 1495) 36. A minor painter who settled at Siena sometime before 1452 and developed under the joint influence of Sassetta and Vecchietta. His works have a naive, provincial charm. Chief amongst them are *The Massacre of the Innocents*, in several versions, and a number of altarpieces.

MAXENTIUS 21, 57, 74-77.
MEDICI Lorenzo de' 11.

MICHELANGELO, decorations in the Sistine Chapel 85.
Milan, Pinacoteca di Brera 4, 26, 108, 109.
MILANESI Gaetano 35, 107.
Modena, Biblioteca Estense, *Bible of Borso d'Este* 24.
MONTEFELTRO Federigo da (Gubbio, Umbria 1422 - 1482) 14, 21, 26, 46, 93, 97-101, 108, 109.
Natural son of Guidantonio, Count of Montefeltro and Urbino, he became the ruler of Urbino after the death of his half-brother Oddantonio in 1444. A prototype of the condottiere, shrewd and practical in his judgments, courageous and cautious in war, he served in turn the Sforzas, the Aragons, the Pope, and even the antipapal clique, and still succeeded in tripling the size of his dominions, located between San Marino and Gubbio. A man of learning, taste and culture, he made his court a select meeting-place of artists, writers and philosophers. He founded the richest library in western Europe and called in Melozzo da Forli, Justus of Ghent, Pedro Berruguete and the sculptor Domenico Rossellini to decorate his palace at Urbino, designed by the Dalmatian architect Luciano Laurana. He was the lifelong friend and patron of Piero della Francesca. Known as a dispenser of justice and a man of his word.
MONTEFELTRO Guidobaldo da 26, 27; Oddantonio da 46.
Murano 17.

NICODEMUS, Gospel of 72.

PACIOLI Luca (Borgo San Lorenzo ca. 1445 - after 1509) 110.
Mathematician and author of several treatises, he was first a tutor in a

family of rich Venetian merchants. Then, taking orders as a Franciscan, he became a professor of mathematics in different Italian towns. At the court of Ludovico il Moro at Milan, he stood on friendly terms with Leonardo da Vinci. Also a close friend of Piero della Francesca and Leon Battista Alberti. His *Divina Proportione*, written in 1496, reflects many of his friends' ideas. The Venice edition of 1503 contained polyhedral figures drawn in perspective by Leonardo. He also left a *Libellus Corporum Regularium*, which obviously owed a great deal to Piero.

PERINO da Monterchi, Romana di (Piero's mother) 24.

Perugia 27.

PERUGINO (Città del Pieve, Umbria ca. 1445 - Fontignano, near Perugia 1523) 82, 90.
His real name was Pietro Vannucci; called Perugino after the town of Perugia, where he lived for many years. According to Vasari, he studied under Piero della Francesca at Arezzo. At Florence in 1472, where he worked in Verrocchio's bottega and saw pictures by the Flemish painters, whose technique he assimilated. Painted countless pictures for Florence, Rome, Perugia, and the towns of the Marches, and worked at Bologna, Cremona, Pavia and Venice. With Cosimo Rosselli, Botticelli and Ghirlandajo, he was commissioned to decorate the Sistine Chapel in Rome in 1481; many of these frescos were destroyed to make way for Michelangelo. With young Raphael as one of his assistants, he finished the frescos in the Collegio del Cambio at Perugia in 1500. Thereafter his output ran high and its quality fell off.

PIERO DELLA FRANCESCA, treatises: *De Prospectiva Pingendi* 13, 16, 27, 102; *De Quinque Corporibus Regularibus* 13, 26, 27, 102.

Paintings: *Annunciation* (gonfalon) 25, 27; *The Baptism of Christ* 14, 21, 29, 36-39, 102; *Diptych of Federigo da Montefeltro and Battista Sforza* 14, 21, 26, 93, 97-101; *The Flagellation* 15, 16, 26, 29, 46-50; *The Nativity* 93, 104-107; *Polyptych of the Misericordia* 23, 24, 29-35; *The Crucifixion* 31, 34, 35; *Madonna della Misericordia* 30-33; *The Resurrection* 17, 93-96; *St Jerome and a Donor*, *Girolamo Amadi* 29, 40, 41; *St Sigismund worshipped by Sigismondo Pandolfo Malatesta* 29, 42-45; *Virgin Annunciate* 17; *Virgin and Child with Saints and Angels* 4, 93, 108, 110; *Virgin and Child with two Angels* 93, 102-104; *Story of the True Cross* 8, 51-92; *The Annunciation* 57, 59, 63, 77, 92, 104; *The Carrying of the Wood of the Cross* 57; *Death of Adam* 20, 57-62; *The Dream of Constantine* 57, 59, 63, 72, 73; *The Finding of the Cross* 14, 57, 58, 63, 78, 80; *Heraclius restoring the Cross to Jerusalem* 21, 57, 58, 63, 88, 89, 91; *Prophet* 8, 57, 63; *The Queen of Sheba being received by King Solomon* 16, 57, 58, 60, 65, 67-71; *The Queen of Sheba worshipping the Wood of the Cross* 57, 64, 66, 68; *The Revealing of the True Cross* 57, 78, 79, 81; *The Torture of Judas* 57; *The Victory of Constantine over Maxentius* 21, 57, 62, 74-77; *The Victory of Heraclius over Chosroes* 21, 57, 63, 82-87.

PIETRO Nicolò di 41.
PII DI CESENA, Manfredo de' 46.
Pisa, Church of the Carmine 35.

PISANELLO Antonio (1397? - after 1450) 19.
His real name was Antonio Pisano, as he was of Pisan origin. Never staying in one place long, he went from one court to another over the length and breadth of Italy. As a youth he worked at Venice. About 1422 we find him at Mantua, employed by the Gonzagas; shortly afterwards he went to Verona, then to Rome. Having shared in the abortive attempt of Piccinino and Francesco Gonzaga to capture Verona in 1439, he was obliged to seek refuge at Venice, though in exchange for protection the Venetian governement sternly forbade him to return to Mantua and Verona. In time he was allowed to go to Ferrara, but it was a good many years before he saw Verona again. From 1443 on he divided his time between Ferrara and Mantua, then moved on to Rimini and, about 1448, to Naples. As well as a great painter, Pisanello was the finest medalist of the Renaissance, and art patrons and connoisseurs vied for his services. His art links up with the International Gothic style, to which he gave a highly refined, poetic expression all his own. Unfortunately few of his works have survived, the best of these being the large fresco of *St George* (Church of Sant' Anastasia, Verona), the decorations on the tomb of Niccolo Brenzoni (Church of San Fermo, Verona), *The Vision of St Eustace* (National Gallery, London) the portrait of Lionello d'Este (Accademia Carrara, Bergamo), the portrait of a princess (Louvre, Paris), as well as a number of medals and drawings, notably in the *Codice Vallardi* (Louvre).

PLATO 14.

PLOTINUS 12.
POLLAIOLO Antonio (Florence ca. 1432 - Rome 1498) 17, 21.
His real name was Antonio di Jacopo Benci, but his father was a poulterer, hence the nickname of Pollaiolo. Most of his works were carried out in collaboration with his brother Piero. Painter, draftsman, engraver, architect, sculptor and goldsmith, Antonio produced fine works in every medium, but unfortunately few of them have survived. He is known to have painted three large pictures of *The Labours of Hercules*, but no trace of them remains. He made cartoons for 27 embroideries on *The Life of St John the Baptist* for the Baptistery, Florence. In 1467 he began work on a funerary monument in the Church of San Miniato, Florence. At Rome he made the figurines of *Romulus and Remus and the She-Wolf*, emblem of the Eternal City, and the bronze tombs of Popes Sixtus IV and Innocent VIII in St Peter's. Among his best-known paintings are *The Martyrdom of St Sebastian* and *Apollo and Daphne* (both in the National Gallery, London), *The Rape of Dejanira* (Jarves Collection, New Haven), and a *Portrait of a Woman* (Museo Poldi-Pezzoli, Milan).

QUIRIACUS, Bishop of Jerusalem (see JUDAS).

ROBINSON, Sir J. C. 36.
Rome 23, 25, 68, 77, 85.
ROSINI 96.
ROTONDI P. 108.
RUMOHR Von, *Italienische Forschungen*
90.

SALMI Mario 24, 35.

SALUTATI Coluccio (Stignano in Val-
dinievole, Tuscany 1331 - Florence
1406) 11.
After studying both literature and
law, he elected for public life and
held offices at Todi (1367), Lucca
(1371), and in the meantime at
Viterbo as one of the apostolic secre-
taries of Pope Urban V. He rose to
the position of Bishop, then left the
orders and in 1375 was appointed
Chancelor of the Signoria at Florence, then in the throes of partisan
strife between Guelfs and Ghibellines.
But his fairness and integrity were
recognized on all sides and he remained in office until his death. Not only
a distinguished statesman, Salutati
was regarded as the greatest scholar
of his day after the deaths of Petrarch
(1374) and Boccaccio (1375). He
retrieved and edited many ancient
manuscripts. The best of his own
writings is in his letters and his treatises. In the cathedral at Fiesole is
a bust of Salutati, made by Mino
da Fiesole about 1466.

SANTI GIOVANNI (Raphael's father)
26.
SETH (son of Adam) 72.
SFORZA Battista 14, 21, 26, 43, 97-101.
SHEBA, Queen of 10, 14, 16, 21, 57,
58, 60, 64-72.
Siena 18.
Siloam (stream) 72, 77.
SIGISMUND St 25, 29, 42-45.

SIGNORELLI Luca 96.
Sinigallia,Church of Santa Maria delle
Grazie 102.
SOLOMON, King 16, 57, 58, 60, 65,
67-69, 72, 74.

Torcello 17.
Tuscany 19, 82.

Umbria 82.
Urbino 15, 16, 23, 26, 27, 46, 50, 97,
102, 104, 108; Castle 108; Cathedral 50; Church of San Bernardino
26, 108; Church of San Donato
108; Galleria Nazionale delle Marche 46-49, 102, 103.
UZIELLI Matthew 36.

VAN DER GOES Hugo (Ghent? -
Rouge Cloître, near Brussels 1482)
Portinari Triptych 104.
A document in the Louvain archives
mentions him as a native of Ghent,
where in fact, in 1467, he was appointed head of the Painters' Guild. At
Bruges in 1468, where he made decorations for the wedding of Charles the
Bold and Margaret of York. In 1475
he was commissioned to paint a large
altarpiece for Tommaso Portinari,
commercial agent of the Medici family at the port of Bruges; in a chapel
of the hospital of Santa Maria Nuova
at Florence for over 400 years,
the *Portinari Triptych* is now in the
Uffizi. In 1476 he withdrew to a
monastery near Brussels, known as
the Rouge Cloître, where he worked
on actively until his death. A restless,
experimental-minded artist, he deeply
influenced 15th-century painting.

VAN EYCK Jan (Gelderland ca. 1385-
1390 - Bruges 1441) 102.
First mentioned in 1422 at The
Hague, where he worked until 1424

for John of Bavaria, Count of Holland. By special decree, dated May 19, 1425, he was appointed Court Painter to the Duke of Burgundy, in whose service he remained until his death. The Duke, Philip the Good, treated him with the utmost esteem and generosity, and entrusted him with several confidential missions. On an embassy to Portugal in 1428 he painted two portraits of the Infanta Isabella, bride of the Duke in 1429. Upon his return Van Eyck settled at Bruges, where, in the course of the next seven years, he painted his finest works, notably his great altarpiece, *The Adoration of the Mystic Lamb* (Church of St Bavon, Ghent), a work traditionally begun by his brother Hubert, whose actual existence, however, is now doubted. Jan van Eyck left several signed works and others identifiable by their inscriptions. His importance in the history of painting is incalculable, both from the technical and stylistic points of view.

VASARI Giorgio (Arezzo 1511 - Florence 1574) 24, 27, 35, 86, 96, 107. Painter, architect and writer. Sent to Florence as a youth to study painting, he worked under Michelangelo, whom he worshipped as a god, then under Andrea del Sarto and Baccio Bandinelli. After a stay at Arezzo, he went to Rome in 1531, where he studied the works of Michelangelo and Raphael, and also took up sculpture and architecture, on which Michelangelo advised him to concentrate. Traveled widely in Italy and at the suggestion of Cardinal Farnese, his patron, decided to write his *Lives of the Best Painters, Sculptors and Architects*. The first edition came out in March 1550. Setting at Florence in 1554, he was commissioned to restore the Palazzo Vecchio and to build the Uffizi (intended as an office building for the magistrature). Much in demand as an architect and painter, he restored the churches of Santa Croce and Santa Maria Novella " in the modern manner " and began the long passage-way linking the Palazzo Pitti to the Palazzo Vecchio. A second edition of his *Lives* came out in 1568. In 1570 he painted frescos in several chapels of the Vatican and completed those he had begun in the Palazzo Vecchio, Florence. We find an abundance of information about Vasari in his own *Letters* and in his autobiography in the *Lives*.
Vatican, Sistine Chapel 85 ; Stanze 85.
Venice 18, 19, 41, 43 ; Galleria dell' Accademia 40, 41, 43.
VENTURI Adolfo, *Piero della Francesca* 97.
Verona 26.

VORAGINE Jacopo (Genoa ca. 1230 - 1298 or 1299). 72.
Italian churchman and writer of sermons and chronicles. Active as a Dominican preacher in different parts of Italy, he rose rapidly in the Order and became a favorite of Pope Nicholas IV, who made him Archbishop of Genoa in 1292. His *Golden Legend*, one of the most popular books of the Middle Ages, is a collection of very quaint accounts saints' lives. of Translated into French as early as the 14th century, it was also one of the earliest books to come from the printing press ; Caxton translated and printed it, with 70 woodcuts, in 1483.

WARBURG, *Acts of the Tenth International Congress of the History of Art* 68.

CONTENTS

HIS WORKS

CHAPTER ONE

CHAPTER TWO

THIS VOLUME

THE SIXTH OF THE COLLECTION

THE TASTE OF OUR TIME

WAS PRINTED
BOTH TEXT AND COLORPLATES
BY THE

COLOR STUDIO

AT IMPRIMERIES RÉUNIES S.A. LAUSANNE

FINISHED THE THIRTY-FIRST DAY OF MARCH
NINETEEN HUNDRED AND FIFTY-FOUR

The works reproduced in this volume were photographed by

Hans Hinz, Basel
(pages 3, 8, 42, 44, 52, 59 |62, 64|67, 69|71, 73|76, 78|81, 83|89, 91, 92, 100)
Claudio Emmer, Milan
(pages 30, 33, 34, 40, 45, 47, 48, 49, 95, 96, 98, 99, 101, 103, 109),
and Louis Laniepce, Paris
(pages 37, 38, 39, 105, 106, 107)

The colorplates were engraved by Guezelle et Renouard, Paris